# Christianity and
# Western Literature

# Christianity and Western Literature
## A Story of Sin and Salvation

Ambrose Mong

James Clarke & Co.

James Clarke & Co.

P.O. Box 60
Cambridge
CB1 2NT
United Kingdom

www.jamesclarke.co
publishing@jamesclarke.co

Paperback ISBN: 978 0 227 17941 3
PDF ISBN: 978 0 227 17943 7
ePub ISBN: 978 0 227 17942 0

*British Library Cataloguing in Publication Data*
A record is available from the British Library

First published by James Clarke & Co., 2023

Copyright © Ambrose Mong, 2023

All rights reserved. No part of this edition may be reproduced, stored electronically or in any retrieval system, or transmitted in any form or by any means, electronic, mechanical, photocopying, recording, or otherwise, without prior written permission from the Publisher (permissions@jamesclarke.co).

*In Memory of Father Bonifacio Solís OP*
(1945 to 2021)

*The Church as a body has never made up her mind about the Arts*
Dorothy L. Sayers

# Contents

*Preface and Acknowledgements*   ix

Introduction   1

Chapter 1   *Confessions*   5
Augustine of Hippo (354-430)

Chapter 2   *The Divine Comedy*   26
Dante Alighieri (1265-1321)

Chapter 3   *Hamlet* and *The Tempest*   50
William Shakespeare (1564-1616)

Chapter 4   *Paradise Lost*   73
John Milton (1608-1674)

Chapter 5   *The Rime of the Ancient Mariner*   95
Samuel Taylor Coleridge (1772-1834)

Chapter 6   *The Brothers Karamazov*   114
Fyodor Dostoevsky (1821-1881)

Chapter 7   *The Power and the Glory*   133
Graham Greene (1904-1991)

Conclusion   152

*Bibliography*   157

*Index*   167

# Preface and Acknowledgements

As a child, I often read the lives of the saints, which captured my imagination. They were like superheroes, fighting evil forces and rescuing people from darkness and ignorance through their learning, prayer and good works. These lives are collectively known as hagiography and saints are people the Catholic Church has canonised. But in literature, saints could also include those who, through their sacrifice and struggle, lived an exemplary life of holiness. These stories are the best form of literature to inculcate faith, especially in young children. Saints inspire us and serve as role models. Saints are not marble statues, but writings about these selected few can inspire believers and lead others to the faith. Many people I know have been converted to Christianity through reading just one book which resonates with their spiritual aspirations.

This book emerged from the Christianity and Western Literature course I taught at The Chinese University of Hong Kong in 2021. Most undergraduates in that class majored in Religious Studies, but only some had adequate knowledge of Christianity. Nonetheless, by reading some of the texts discussed here, the students gained deeper comprehension of Christian belief and gospel values conveyed in different contexts and historical periods. Conceivably, fiction, poems and plays can be powerful tools in portraying the Christian faith in action. Perhaps the decline in Christianity in the West is due to the lack of reading good literature.

Many people have assisted me in this project. Special thanks to Denis Chang SC for collaborating to write the chapter on Dante Alighieri, *The Divine Comedy*. Kenzie Lau has been a great source of support in her editorial assistance and suggestions. I am also grateful to Br Patrick Tierney FSC, Sr Mary Gillis CND, Dr Doris Kin-Mee Au for proofreading the text, and Jane Robson for her excellent copy-editing. Thanks to the Parish Priest of St Joseph's Church, Revd Joseph Tan SVD, and my fellow colleague, Revd Paul Chan SVD, for their care and fellowship. Special thanks to Bishop Stephen Chow SJ who has approved my sabbatical leave so that I could complete this work.

Finally, I am very grateful to Adrian Brink, the managing director, Samuel Fitzgerald, the editor, and the dedicated staff at James Clarke & Co. for bringing this modest work into print. Any errors that remain are, of course, my own.

Ambrose Mong<br>
St Joseph's Church<br>
Hong Kong

# Introduction

Throughout history, the Church has been cautious regarding literary works, having condemned and condoned, suppressed as well as supported works of art. Some writers have adopted a positive attitude towards literature, seeing it as a channel to convey the Christian vision. Others regard literature as hostile to Christian belief, misleading the faithful.

Rooted in the teaching of Paul, the early Church was clearly critical towards literature. Paul teaches that Christians should not compromise with worldly attitudes and values such as those propagated by pagan writings: 'Do not be mismatched with unbelievers. For what partnership is there between righteousness and lawlessness? Or what fellowship is there between light and darkness? What agreement does Christ have with Beliar? Or what does a believer share with an unbeliever?' (2 Corinthians 6:14-15). However, Paul was a learned man, familiar with the ancient classics. During his speech delivered at the Areopagus in Athens, he referred to Cleanthes, Aratus and Epimenides, who was also critical of the people of Crete: 'For "In him we live and move and have our being"; as even some of your own poets have said, "For we too are his offspring."' (Acts 17:28; Titus 1:12-13). In some of his writings, Paul also alluded to Homer and Plato.[1]

Be that as it may, the classical culture is fraught with contradiction regarding the function of literature. Plato had banned poets from his republic, a policy which Augustine approved wholeheartedly. According to Augustine, the poets 'composed fictions with no regard to the truth or set the worst possible examples before wretched people under the

---

1. Alister E. McGrath, *Christian Literature: An Anthology* (Oxford: Blackwell Publishers, 2001), p. xi.

pretence that they were divine actions'.[2] However, Paul's speeches and Augustine's writing were steeped in Aristotelian rhetoric.

The attitude of early Christians towards literature was rather ambivalent and nuanced. Early Church Fathers such as Tertullian and Chrysostom were critical of classical literature and sought to minimise their influence within the Christian community. Augustine and Jerome were cautious but also positive towards pagan writings. Christian apologists could see the advantage of literature, with its beauty of expression, to spread the gospel message. Literature can serve to clarify and communicate abstract theological viewpoints. Thus, if people enjoy reading fiction and poetry, it makes sense to present religious truth in literary forms.

For C.S. Lewis, reading has always been a religious experience. Literary insight is like worship where he can transcend and experience himself as he truly is.

> The first reading of some literary work is often, to the literary, an experience so momentous that only experience of love, religion, or bereavement can furnish a standard of comparison. Their whole consciousness is changed. They have become what they were not before. But there is no sign of anything like this among the other sort of readers. When they have the story or the novel, nothing much or nothing at all, seems to have happened to them.[3]

Writers during the Romantic period argued that the language of literature could inspire readers to devotion and piety. William Wordsworth believed that there is a close affinity between poetry and religion; thus his poems are infused with religious and spiritual symbolism. Writers during Wordsworth's time began to see the Bible as literature. In fact, Percy Bysshe Shelley held that the Scripture is revered more for its literary quality than for its spiritual value.

The 'Word' has always been important in Christian teaching. According to John's Gospel: 'In the beginning was the Word, and the Word was with God, and the Word was God' (1:1). Thus with 'God as author', there is a close connection between the verbal origin of the world and the world of texts. Christian literature can help to teach a

---

2. Quoted in McGrath, *Christian Literature*, p. xi.
3. Quoted in Lawrence Wood, 'Seeing with a Thousand Eyes', *The Christian Century* 122, no. 10 (2005), p. 7.

set of beliefs such as the Creed, doctrines and sermons. It can also help to inculcate values such as compassion, tolerance and forgiveness. The *lives* of saints, or hagiographies, have played important roles within the church in nurturing and inspiring the faithful. As the 'religion of the book', Christian faith involves extensive use of texts to communicate its message, educate its members and defend its beliefs. Hence, spiritual writings, as a form of literature, can also promote a way of life in accordance with the gospel vision and play a fundamental role in passing the tenets of Christianity from generation to generation.

This work explores the relationship between Christianity and Western literature, with a selection of authors representative of each epoch, from late antiquity, Augustine of Hippo (354-430); the Middle Ages, Dante Alighieri (1265-1321); the Renaissance, William Shakespeare (1564-1616) and John Milton (1608-74); the Romantic period, Samuel Taylor Coleridge (1772-1834); and the modern era, Fyodor Dostoevsky (1821-81) and Graham Greene (1904-91). Exploring the motif of the fall and redemption of humanity, this book examines the themes of creation, sin, suffering, forgiveness, hell, purgatory and heaven.

Augustine's *Confessions*, Dante's *Divine Comedy* and Milton's *Paradise Lost* were written specially to serve the needs of the Christian community. Each a product of its period, their writings all represent a high standard of cultural and scholarly excellence. Shakespeare's *Hamlet* and *The Tempest* and Coleridge's *The Rime of the Ancient Mariner*, though not specific to the Christian faith, have been profoundly influenced by Christian ideas, values, images and narrative. In Dostoevsky's *The Brothers Karamazov* and Greene's *The Power and the Glory*, the influence of Christianity is evident in their subject matter. Their novels also challenge and question Christian assumptions by portraying the conflict and tension between the priestly and prophetic understanding of the faith. Written in the modern period, these texts, while defending the truth of Christianity, are critical of the materialism, secularism and socialism prevalent in their societies.

# Chapter 1

## *Confessions*

### Augustine of Hippo (354-430)

Augustine of Hippo, one of the greatest Christian writers in Christianity and especially in the Western Church, was born in Thagaste, a seaport in North Africa, part of the Roman province of Numidia (present-day Algeria). As he was a precocious child, his parents, Patricius and Monica, made great sacrifices for his education and had high hopes for him. Monica, a devout Christian, prayed hard to inculcate him with her faith. Augustine, however, did not take his mother's faith seriously. At the age of 17, he took a mistress and had a son with her. At 19, he came under the influence of Manichaeism, a gnostic sect, but left after nine years as a member.

He taught rhetoric in Thagaste, Carthage, Rome and Milan. Augustine eventually settled in Italy and joined the Roman civil service. While in Milan, he underwent a conversion experience in July 386 and was baptised by Ambrose, Bishop of Milan (339-97). This renowned conversion is narrated in his most famous work, *Confessions*.

Augustine returned to his home town in North Africa in 388. Although considering himself unworthy, he was ordained a priest in the coastal town of Hippo Regius in 391 and became a bishop in 395. Besides administering the affairs of the local church in North Africa, Augustine was also busy writing in defence of the Christian faith against various heresies such as Manichaeism, Donatism and Pelagianism, and these works later shaped and defined orthodox Christian doctrines. He pursued constructive engagement and dialogue with Western classical philosophy, poetry and rhetoric. Augustine is credited with developing the genre of autobiography in the *Confessions*, as a means of praising God and inspiring others in the faith. His psychological insight and dramatic expressions of intellectual doubt and moral weakness made him one of the most compelling authors in Christian history. Influencing many writers throughout the ages, Augustine's dramatic conversion and theological insight contributed to the advancement of Christian literature.

Oddly enough, Augustine was critical and mistrustful of literature, especially fiction, for its power to seduce and mislead. Regarding the theatre he wrote, 'How is it that a man wants to be made sad by the sight of tragic sufferings that he could not bear in his own person? Yet the spectator does want to feel sorrow and it is the feeling of his sorrow that he enjoys.'[1] Literature allows us to feel sadness without undergoing that experience and thus removes us from the truth. Augustine also recognised the importance of storytelling in leading us to the truth about God and human existence. In fact, he developed a literary form that subsequent prominent authors have followed. It became the framework of *Confessions*, a narrative recounting a restless journey from childhood to adult spiritual maturity after undergoing a conversion experience. This idea that narrating one's life story can lead to spiritual enlightenment has influenced literature ever since.[2]

Autobiography was very much part of the Roman literary tradition, with tales of individuals searching for truth amid worldly temptations. The publication of Augustine's *Confessions* between 397 and 400, however, was considered ground-breaking in Latin literature in that it dealt with introspection and the development of the soul. Christian biographies were popular in the early Church, for example, St Athanasius's *Life of Antony*, Jerome's *De Viris Illustribus*, Cyprian's *To Donatus*, Justin Martyr's *Dialogue with Trypho*, and the treatise *On the Trinity* by Hilary of Poitiers. Focussing on present trials, such as imprisonment and martyrdom, most of these accounts are relatively short and lack the depth of introspection exhibited in Augustine's *Confessions*. During his time,

---

1. *Confessions* 3.2, pp. 37–38. All quotations are taken from F.J. Sheed, trans., *Confessions*, 2nd ed., with notes by Michael P. Foley (Indianapolis, IN: Hackett Publishing Co., 2006).
2. Robert Peter Kennedy, Kim Paffenroth, John Doody and Marylin Hill, 'Introduction', in Robert Peter Kennedy, Kim Paffenroth and John Doody (eds.), *Augustine and Literature* (Lanham, MD: Lexington Books, 2006), p. 1.

the Church became firmly established in Roman society. The enemies of Christianity were no longer seen as coming from outside but rather as being inside the individual. The peak of the person's life would not be dying but living for God, not martyrdom but conversion. Augustine's *Confessions* represents the best in the tradition of religious autobiography in which we 'witness the stages of human cooperation with transforming grace',[3] teaching us to transcend.

This chapter explores Augustine's teaching on creation and sin in *Confessions*, which in many ways emerged out of the influence of Manichaeism upon him, and also his refutation of it. It was also supported by his reading of Neoplatonism and the Pauline epistles. According to J. Kevin Coyle, 'Manichaeism formed for Augustine the conscious foil against which he measured his Christian orthodoxy, affecting the choice of the themes he worked with and how he dealt with them.'[4] Without his encounter with Manichaeism, as a follower and also as a foe, Augustine's theology would be very different, for most of his works were polemical and pastoral pieces written against this backdrop. He might have left Manichaeism, but Manichaeism never totally left him. Augustine's reading of Neoplatonism, whose veracity could be supported by the scriptural authority of St Paul, and the influence of Ambrose, Bishop of Milan, eventually led him to be reconciled with Christianity. *Confessions* is about his return to Christianity rather than a conversion.

## Manichaeism

Mani, the founder of Manichaeism, was born in Mesopotamia (present-day Iraq) in 216. Convinced that he had a revelation from God, superseding other religious founders, Mani established the 'Religion of Light', a fusion of elements drawn from Buddhism, Zoroastrianism and gnostic Christianity. It rejected the Old Testament and claimed to be authentic Christianity, spreading across Egypt, northwest Africa, the Roman Empire and even China. Mani regarded himself as the 'apostle of Christ', the Paraclete that Jesus had promised. A threat to Christianity and native religion, Mani was attacked by Zoroastrian priests and died in prison in 274.

---

3. Quoted in Janet Taylor, 'The Confessions of St Augustine: A Spiritual Classic', *Crux* 21, no. 3 (1985), p. 19.
4. John Kevin Coyle, *Manichaeism and its Legacy* (Leiden and Boston: Brill, 2009), p. xxi.

Central to Manichaeism is the problem of evil, which Mani attempted to resolve by a myth regarding a pre-cosmic battle between powers of light and darkness. Mani maintained that fragments of divine light are captured by the evil powers of darkness that remain in the physical bodies of human beings. This divine light could be liberated by adhering to Manichaean rites, doctrine and diet. Mani presented his cosmogony, an explanation of the origin of the universe, in three phases: first, good (spirit and light) and evil (matter and darkness) have separate and distinct existences; secondly, in the present state good and evil are intermingled; thirdly, good and evil return to their separate existence. Thus, the two principles of good and evil are completely separated in the beginning. However, during the second phase, the evil principle invaded the good principle and trapped the light in darkness. God caused the evil principle to create the visible world out of this fusion to liberate the light from darkness. God himself also created a planetary system of sun and moon to collect any light released from darkness and eventually return to the good principle.[5]

Manichaeism asserts that Adam and Eve were created not by God but by an evil initiative, the union of demons, to keep the light trapped in the material world. Each human being is a microcosm in which the primordial battle between matter and light takes place. The person can be saved by removing himself from this cosmic chaos, which requires special knowledge given only to the Elect, the 'perfect ones', who heard the call and responded to it. The Elect are elite members of Manichaeism who followed a special diet, practised asceticism and celibacy, and prayed regularly. The other members are the Hearers (catechumens), whose primary duty is to serve the Elects. They could own property and get married, but procreation was discouraged.[6]

The Hearers' hope is to be reborn as one of the Elect, while the destiny of the 'Elect' is to recover their light substance and return to their rightful place. This will happen during the third phase, when much light has been released through the effort of the Elects. After that, the physical world will disappear, and the evil substance will return to the dark realm, once more separated from the light. Nevertheless, some of the light remained trapped in darkness forever.[7] This esoteric religion that regards matter and creation as evil fascinated the young and restless Augustine.

---

5. Coyle, *Manichaeism and Its Legacy*, p. xiv.
6. Coyle, *Manichaeism and Its Legacy*, pp. xiv–xv.
7. Coyle, *Manichaeism and Its Legacy*, p. xv.

As a Hearer, Augustine was familiar with Manichaeism's teaching, methods and practices. He had to serve food to the 'elect and holy, that in the factory of their stomachs they should turn it into angels and deities by whom I was to be set free'.[8] Truth attainable by reason without faith was given to its founder, Mani, who had chosen the Elect to mediate between God and human beings. One may wonder how such a religion with its bizarre myth and absurd dietary regulations appeared credible to a highly intelligent young man like Augustine. He remained a Hearer for a staggering nine years!

Manichaeism's claim to be an authentic version of Christianity might have led Augustine to believe that it could help him to understand the Bible better. This new religion offered him justification for his ongoing sexual relations. With their interest in astrology, a community of believers assured him of friendship and support. Most importantly, the Manicheans taught Augustine that he could discover the truth through reason, and solve the problem of good and evil.

## Origin of Evil

The eclectic teaching of Manichaeism appealed to Augustine because it offered answers to his questions regarding the nature of the divine and the problem of evil. This gnostic philosophy holds that evil does not come from God but from a separate substance that has invaded and captured the good. Not limited to human shape, God is 'a luminous immeasurable body', while the person is 'a kind of particle broken from that body'.[9] Thus the goodness of human beings is assaulted by the evil substance.

By adopting Manichaeism, which asserts that the forces of evil could not harm the good soul, Augustine finds justification in avoiding guilt. The soul remains untarnished because it contains elements of divine substance, as it were. Thus, as a Manichaean, Augustine found consolation even as he struggled to find the self-discipline to leave his mistress, which was a grave concern for his mother. This moral strain of Manichaeism appears as a consolation or justification for his waywardness:

> For I still held the view that it was not we that sinned, but some other nature sinning in us; and it pleased my pride to

---

8. *Confessions*, 4.1.1, p. 55.
9. *Confessions*, 4.16.31, p. 72.

> be beyond fault, and when I did any evil not to confess that I had done it, that You might heal my soul because it had sinned against You. I very much preferred to excuse myself and accuse some other thing that was in me but was not I.

Nonetheless, he was willing to acknowledge that the impiety that caused him to offend against God was 'wholly I'.[10]

Initially, Augustine's ego was attracted to a rational and dualistic philosophy that exonerates the good soul from sin. Presenting itself as genuine Christianity, Manichaeism drew him:

> Here are all the elements that attract him: idealistic thought, aesthetic leanings, a richly developed symbolism, and a carefully nurtured mysticism. With this, for 'the initiated', comes the privileged enjoyment of higher knowledge. And one final point: in Manichaeism – as in every gnosis – the genuinely ethical is dissolved in the cosmic; evil simply becomes part of world happening, thus mitigating personal responsibility for it.[11]

Be that as it may, Augustine was rather sceptical about the doctrine that materialism espoused. A dualistic understanding of evil means that the good cannot be accountable for wrongdoings. It also implies that the good is not invincible but could be overcome by the dark forces. Despite this doubt, Augustine remained a member of this sect for nine years until he encountered their famous Manichaean bishop, Faustus, who revealed to him that they did not have all the answers.[12]

Realising that he was misguided, Augustine would refute the erroneous doctrines of Manichaeism from a Christian perspective because it does not make a clear distinction between the creator and his creation. The Manichaeans conceive God, not as a divine being, but as part of the world. Augustine admits: 'When I desired to think of my God, I could not think of Him save as a bodily magnitude, for it seemed to me that what was not such was nothing at all: this indeed was the principal and practically the sole cause of my inevitable error.'[13]

---

10. *Confessions*, 5.10.18, p. 86.
11. Romano Guardini, *The Conversion of Augustine* (Westminster, MD: Newman Press, 1960), p. 170.
12. *Confessions*, 5.712, p. 82.
13. *Confessions*, 5.19.19, pp. 87–88.

Manichaean teaching maintains that God and the world make up the whole cosmic reality while the divine element, though highest, remains part of the universe.

If God is part of the cosmos, Augustine concludes that the Manichaean deity is corruptible. God is not transcendental and distinct, but just another being in the world, mingled with contrary powers of light and darkness.[14] Manichaeism maintains that the human soul, a member of God, a part of divine substance, is under attack by the body, identified as the evil matter. A person has two eternal principles, representing the whole cosmic reality. Augustine also holds that each person is a microcosm with spiritual and physical elements, but this being is ontologically distinct from God, the creator, whereas in Manichaeism, God and human beings are conflated.

Augustine believes that this denial of the distinction between God and his creation leads humans to be proud. They would like to be the light, not in the Lord, but in themselves, as they imagine 'the nature of the soul to be the same as God'.[15] Rejecting moral responsibility, this arrogance leads to the denial that humans are culpable and responsible for their sins, and to the belief that they are merely victims of the cosmic conflict between good and evil.[16]

## Ambrose of Milan

Incidentally, another bishop from the Catholic Church, Ambrose, Bishop of Milan, provided Augustine with the answers that prepared his way to embrace Christianity wholeheartedly. Augustine writes: 'Faustus was simply straying about among the fallacies of the Manichees, Ambrose taught the doctrine of salvation most profitably.'[17] A Roman aristocrat, Ambrose was a profound theologian and gifted orator who received Augustine 'as a father' and 'as a bishop' with kindness.[18] Ambrose's eloquent preaching attracted Augustine to attend services regularly.

Ambrose, who was prominent in the Christian community, thus represented the Church for Augustine. Known for his allegorical

---

14. *Confessions*, 7.2.3, pp. 118–19.
15. *Confessions*, 7.1022, p. 155.
16. See Samuel N. C. Lieu, *Manichaeism in the Later Roman Empire and Medieval China*, 2nd rev. and expanded ed. (Tübingen: J.C.B. Mohr, 1992), pp. 25, 117–53.
17. *Confessions*, 5.13.23, p. 91.
18. *Confessions*, 5.13.23, p. 90.

interpretation of the Scriptures, Ambrose greatly influenced Augustine in accepting the Church as a teacher and as a place of grace and healing. The practice of celibacy and monastic observances in Ambrose's life sharply contrasted with the mechanical piety and vainglory that Augustine had come to associate with the Church. Augustine learned from Ambrose to accept the Church as a teaching authority on faith and morals, and at the same time, to accept personal responsibility for one's soul. A Pauline scholar, Ambrose impressed Augustine with a clear sense of personal sin and the importance of grace.

## Pauline Influence

In *Confessions*, we read that when the African civil servant Ponticianus visited Augustine in Milan, 'he noticed a book on a gaming table … he picked it up, opened it, and found that it was the Apostle Paul, which surprised him'.[19] Ponticianus was a devout Christian. He narrated to Augustine the story of the Egyptian monk Antony, and the conversion and renunciation of his two friends when they encountered this work. Later, Antony is mentioned again, in the context of Augustine's own conversion, when he heard, 'Take and read, take and read.'[20] Augustine then took up the volume of Paul and read 'let us live honourably as in the day, not in revelling and drunkenness, not in debauchery and licentiousness, not in quarrelling and jealousy. Instead, put on the Lord Jesus Christ, and make no provision for the flesh, to gratify its desires' (Rom. 13:13-14). The reading of Paul and the story of Antony underscores the important role of conversion and renunciation in Augustine's life.

Augustine turns to Paul to reflect on the disputes regarding sin, free will, Jewish law, the merits of faith and works, suffering, grace and justification. Paul's teaching on these questions provided scriptural authority to counteract heretical sects like the Manichaeans, who also venerated the apostle. Actually, Augustine's reading of Paul came indirectly through Manichaean texts and their refutations. Mani's mission was an imitation of Paul, emphasising dualism, the Holy Spirit, the Church and the rejection of Mosaic Law to such an extent that Manichaeism was labelled 'almost a Pauline heresy'.[21] Claiming to be the true Church of Jesus Christ in the tradition of the Pauline churches,

---

19. *Confessions*, 8.6.14, p. 150.
20. *Confessions*, 8.12.29, p. 159.
21. Carol Harrison, *Rethinking Augustine's Early Theology: An Argument for Continuity* (Oxford and New York: Oxford University, 2006), p. 121.

the Manichaeans were 'the most radical and self-confident of Paul's expositors'.[22]

After his conversion, Augustine wrote furiously to reclaim Paul for Catholic Christianity. He read Paul differently from the Manichaeans, focusing on the tension between flesh and spirit, the helplessness of human beings, and their utter dependence on the grace of God. Augustine believed that the Manichaean interpretation of Paul undermines Catholic teaching on salvation. Manichaean dualism contradicts the Christian belief of One God, creator of the world, which Paul himself upheld. Against the Manichaeans, Augustine upheld the undivided Trinity as well as the harmony of the Old Testament and the New Testament. Augustine also heard the true teaching of Paul in the Church, 'And it was a joy to hear Ambrose who often repeated to his congregation, as if it were a rule he was almost strongly urging them to follow; the text: *the letter killeth, but the spirit giveth life*' (2 Cor. 3:6).[23]

Pauline writings do not contradict the Platonists but confirm the truth that Augustine was searching for: 'I found that whatever truth I had read in the Platonists was said here with praise of Your grace: that he who sees should not so glory as if he had not received – and received, indeed, not only what he sees but even the power to see, for what has he that he has not received?'[24] Everything depends on the grace of God, not on our own abilities.

## Neoplatonism

Besides the encounter with Ambrose, the 'books of the Platonists'[25] provided another significant influence in Augustine's spiritual journey. Henry Chadwick puts it succinctly: 'Ambrose has convinced him of the incorporeality of God and preached so profound a fusion of Christianity with Platonic mysticism that Augustine thinks of Christ and Plato as different teachers converging in the same truths, complementary to each other.'[26] Augustine thus began to perceive the nature of the divine as immaterial and the soul as superior to the body, corresponding

---

22. Peter Brown, *Augustine of Hippo: A Biography* (Berkeley and Los Angeles, LA: University of California Press, 1967), p. 151.
23. *Confessions*, 6.4.6, p. 99.
24. *Confessions*, 7.21.27, p. 136.
25. *Confessions*, 7.9.13, p. 126.
26. Henry Chadwick, *Augustine of Hippo: A Life* (Oxford: Oxford University Press, 2009), pp. 29–30.

to Christianity's teaching on God, the immortality of the soul and sin. Understanding Christian belief in the light of Platonism taught Augustine to relate to sin as carnal pleasure and salvation as a liberation from this attachment.

Developed by Plotinus (204/5-270 CE) and his followers, Neoplatonism is the modern name given to this school, although they regarded themselves as 'Platonists'.[27] By interpreting Plato, the philosophy of Plotinus attempts to solve spiritual issues in terms of Hellenistic rationalism. One of the issues is the relationship between cause and effect, which Plotinus calls *non-reciprocating*: 'the higher determines the lower without itself being determined or modified by its causative activity; it communicates its own force, in a diminished degree, to its product, but itself suffers thereby no diminution of force, or change of any kind'.[28] For Plotinus, the individual possesses a will that enables him to realise his true self by self-identification with his source, a 'Return' to the One.

Self-exploration, the idea of self-consciousness, 'the ego's awareness of its own activity', is fundamental to the philosophy of Plotinus.[29] He sees the experience as an 'awakening to myself'. According to Plotinus and influenced by Greek rationalism, a mysticism that reveals the divine to us is achieved through intellectual efforts. However, 'without true virtue all talk of God is but words'.[30] Neoplatonism teaches that the divine is transcendent, eternal and incorruptible. God is thus not subjected to time and space. Further, the Neoplatonists hold that the divine is One through which all things originate. Therefore, evil, which is something negative, 'has no being of its own but is only an absence of good'.[31]

Augustine discovers many parallels between Neoplatonism and Christianity in Plotinus's *Enneads*, such as the One, which is transcendent and the ground of all beings, the concept of Logos and the idea of Trinity. In contrast to the Christian faith, Neoplatonism embraces polytheism, astrology and magic. Nonetheless, it is a sublime system that can complement Christianity in some respects. With Neoplatonism's concept of 'unchangeable Light',[32] Augustine accepts God as a divine

---

27. Brown, *Augustine of Hippo: A Biography*, p. 91.
28. E. R. Dodds, 'Tradition and Personal Achievement in the Philosophy of Plotinus', *Journal of Roman Studies* 50, no. 1–2 (1960), p. 3.
29. Dodds, 'Tradition and Personal Achievement', p. 6.
30. Dodds, 'Tradition and Personal Achievement', p. 7.
31. *Confessions*, 3.712, p. 44.
32. *Confessions*, 7.10.16, p. 128.

spirit not confined to the human body: 'in the Platonists God and his Word are everywhere implied'.³³

The genius of Augustine lies in his ability to utilise Platonic insights in the service of Christianity. Unlike Manichaeism, Platonism provides him with the intellectual tools to understand the problem of evil and to clarify Christian doctrines: 'Augustine is a Christian who subordinates Neoplatonism to his own purposes rather than a Neoplatonist who disguises himself as a Christian theologian.'³⁴ His Platonic approach to his faith is controlled by Christianity. Thus, his conversion to Christianity was not from paganism but a return to the Christian faith of his mother, Monica. The conversion of Augustine was more of a reconciliation than a sudden switch to a new belief.³⁵

In the *Confessions*, Augustine narrates his conversion in stages: his reading of Cicero's *Hortensius*, the influence of Manichaeism, encountering the Academics, his meeting with Ambrose in Milan, his new insight regarding the nature of God and the soul, and how the writings of the Platonists inspired him. Though they inflamed him, Augustine read the Platonists with a critical mind: he questioned, compared their writings with Scriptures, discerned what aspects possessed the truth, and attempted to find out how they converged or diverged from the faith. Reading the Platonists in the light of Christian faith, he was very aware of their errors, especially their polytheistic beliefs. Augustine was also encouraged and inspired by Christian intellectuals well versed in Neoplatonic philosophy such as Simplicianus and Ambrose.

Understanding God's transcendence in the Platonic sense enables Augustine to refute the dualism of Manichaeism. Augustine writes, 'I saw Your unchangeable Light shining over that same eye of my soul, over my mind.'³⁶ It was a superior light that created him. He also writes about the ascent of the soul to God, illuminated by the light of truth, in Neoplatonic terms, an ascent from body to soul culminating in the glimpse of the transcendent which he describes as 'That which is.'³⁷ This insight into the truth of God and his transcendent nature filled Augustine with profound love and awe. The Platonic idea that existence

---

33. *Confessions* 5.2.3, p. 142.
34. Quoted in Mark J. Boone, 'The Role of Platonism in Augustine's 386 Conversion to Christianity', *Religion Compass* 9, no. 5 (2015), p. 155.
35. Harrison, *Rethinking Augustine's Early Theology*, pp. 22–23.
36. *Confessions*, 7.10.16, p. 128.
37. *Confessions*, 7.17.23, p. 133.

is good, and that evil is not a substance but an absence of the good, provided Augustine with an argument against Manichaean dualism; it also taught him the Christian belief in the essential goodness of creation.

## Doctrine of Creation

Upholding a distinctively Christian doctrine of creation that forms the basis of his reflection on the nature of God and sin, Augustine begins *Confessions* by highlighting humankind as part of God's creation: 'He is but a tiny part of all that Thou hast created.'[38] This brief assertion culminates in his most famous line: 'For Thou hast made us for Thyself and our hearts are restless till they rest in Thee.'[39] Our hearts are restless because God has created human beings oriented towards Him. Indeed, creation is the point of departure for the autobiography, and subsequently it illustrates the nature of his faith.[40] Praying to God as a creator, Augustine ends his *Confessions* with three books dealing with the creation story in Genesis.

Supported by Platonic and Christian philosophical traditions, Augustine emphasises the ontological distinction between the creator and his creation; God is not to be perceived as part of the word, but as transcendent to it.[41] This insight allows us to see creation as revelation. Augustine writes: 'in the testimony of the whole creation I had found You, our Creator, and Your Word who is with You and one God with You, by whom You created all things'.[42] Creation reveals who God is: as Paul says, 'Ever since the creation of the world his eternal power and divine nature, invisible though they are, have been understood and seen through the things he has made' (Rom. 1:20).

Augustine teaches that when God is most hidden, he is most present.[43] God is not part of creation, but '*is* absolutely'.[44] If God simply is, then he is perfectly self-reliant, lacking in nothing. Thus, there is no need for God to create because creation adds nothing to God's goodness. He creates freely because he is goodness itself: 'For You created them not out of any need of them but out of the plentitude of Your goodness,

---

38. *Confessions*, 1.1.1, p. 3.
39. *Confessions*, 1.1.1, p. 3.
40. Harrison, *Rethinking Augustine's Early Theology*, p. 114.
41. *Confessions*, 10.6.8–10, pp. 193–94.
42. *Confessions*, 8.1.2, p. 142.
43. *Confessions*, 1.4.4, p. 4.
44. *Confessions*, 13.31.46, p. 318.

shaping and turning them to form though Your joy was not increased by them.[45] This brings us to Augustine's teaching on 'creation out of nothing'.

## Creatio Ex Nihilo

Augustine's understanding of the doctrine of *creatio ex nihilo* (creation out of nothing) has significant implications for how he views the world and his own life. He begins to see life and the whole human existence as a gratuitous gift from God who is love itself. Human beings are thus utterly dependent on God. Augustine states in his autobiography that our response to our creator should be one of thanksgiving and praise.

Augustine speaks of 'heaven of heaven' (*caelum*) as the highest thing in the spiritual realm, a community of the blessed: 'pure mind united in perfect harmony in a binding union of peace with those holy spirits, the citizens of Your City, which is in heaven far above, the heavens we see'.[46] This blessed community is 'our mother' through whom we are born in baptism.[47] Created before time, this 'heaven of heaven' is not co-eternal with the trinitarian God, but partakes in his divinity.[48] Our earthly Church participates and journeys towards this heavenly Jerusalem.

Human beings are made in the image and likeness of God (Gen. 1:27). At the beginning of *Confessions*, Augustine says that all rational creatures are created and ordered intrinsically towards the creator. Human beings with a rational soul are meant to be oriented towards God. As rational beings, they are endowed with a will that has the freedom to turn freely towards God. It is essentially a moral choice. Augustine writes: 'it is good for it to adhere to You always, lest the light it had gained by turning towards You, it might lose by turning away from You, and so fall back into a life similar to the abyss of darkness'.[49] Thus rational creatures should always preserve their ontological make-up by adhering to God.

Augustine asserts that everything that God creates bears *vestigia Trinitatis*, traces of the Trinity. They participate in God's eternal reason and can freely know and love him. After the Fall, human beings turned away from that image of God in which they were originally created, but fortunately, it was never completely lost. Though deformed, the soul

---

45. *Confessions*, 13.4.5, p. 291.
46. *Confessions*, 12.11.12, p. 267.
47. *Confessions*, 12.15.20, p. 270.
48. *Confessions*, 12.9.9, p. 265.
49. *Confessions*, 13.2.3, p. 290.

seeks to reform itself and return to God. Augustine also highlights the distinction between the Trinity and the imprint of the Trinity in everyone.[50] Each person gives us an insight into the nature of God, who at the same time reveals to us what human beings are like. It is the image of God that enlightens the mystery of God and human beings.[51]

## Creation and Sin

In Augustinian theology, sin is to be understood in the context of creation.[52] According to the teaching of Paul, the sinner is the one who prefers creation rather than the creator: 'they exchanged the truth about God for a lie and worshiped and served the creature rather than the Creator' (Rom. 1:25). Sin occurs when the creature begins to deny his dependence on his creator as the source of life. In fact, the creature desires to be like God, distorting the distinction that defines his existence. Augustine makes this dependence of humans on God clear when he says: 'Therefore my soul is as earth without water unto Thee, for just as it cannot of itself illumine itself, so it cannot of itself quench the thirst that it has. For with thee is the fountain of life, and in Thy light we shall see light.'[53] Sin thus occurs when the sinner tacitly denies the distinction between himself and his creator. Rooted in the will, the creature chooses the lesser good and compromises his very existence. When Augustine was a Manichaean, he erroneously identified the creator with his creation. He had to struggle with this temptation throughout his professional and religious life.

In Book 2 of *Confessions*, Augustine narrates the pear-tree incident, a trivial case of stealing fruit, as indeed sinful because it is done with no purpose other than simply enjoying the theft itself. He did not even eat the fruit but threw them to the pigs, 'tasting only my own sin and savouring that with delight'.[54] This occasion of theft helped Augustine to

---

50. *Confessions*, 13.11.12, p. 295.
51. Jared Ortiz, *'You Made Us for Yourself' : Creation in St Augustine's Confessions* (Minneapolis, MN: Fortress Press, 2016), p. 33.
52. The association of lust with creation occurs in the public bath episode when Augustine's father, Patricius, sees how mature he has become and looks forward to having grandchildren. Loving the creature more than the creator, Augustine laments that his father was merely searching for signs of sexual maturity so that he could have grandchildren. *Confessions*, 2.35, p. 27.
53. *Confessions*, 13.16.19, p. 301.
54. *Confessions*, 2.6.12, p. 31.

meditate on the nature of sin in which he sees, as the corruption of the soul, the tendency to abuse free will. There is no reason to steal and thus he concludes that sin is a perversion of reason. Further, sin is committed through an uncontrolled penchant for things of a lesser order and thus unwittingly forsaking truth and goodness.

Reflecting on the senselessness of sin, Augustine realises that he would not have acted alone, but he was encouraged by his accomplices. Thus, the pleasure was not in the pears but in stealing in the company of fellow sinners. This stolen fruit incident reminds us of the Fall, wherein Adam and Eve ate the forbidden fruit. In this original sin, a naive transgression committed by our first parents, we are all caught up in the corruption of the world, which affects all generations, including babies. As a result, Augustine doubts if infants are innocent as he finds them as greedy and selfish as adults. They do no harm because they lack the will and the strength: 'Thus the innocence of children is in the helplessness of their bodies rather than any quality in their minds.'[55] As a baby, he screamed in rage when he did not get what he desired. Augustine observed jealousy and anger in other infants, although they could not clearly express it. Hence, he did not believe that infants are innocent: 'Indeed, I was born guilty, a sinner when my mother conceived me' (Psalm 51).

## Fall of Man

Influenced by Plotinus, Augustine views the Fall as the soul losing its identity, thus becoming 'a partial thing, isolated, full of cares, intent upon the fragment, severed from the whole'.[56] Augustine writes: 'I collect myself out of that broken state in which my being was torn asunder because I was turned away from Thee, the One, and wasted myself upon the many.'[57] For Plotinus, the soul is a cosmic force, and the Fall represents the human condition. For Augustine, the Fall is the soul wandering away from God, which occurs in the person's heart.[58]

Augustine emphasises human bondage as the origin of sin when we lose the power of our free will due to the Fall. We channel this free choice to ourselves and subject ourselves to inordinate desires. The will becomes defective but not completely corrupted. We are free to do good, but we become a slave to sin after the Fall. Originally this free will is to enable

---

55. *Confessions*, 1.7.11, p. 9.
56. Plotinus, *Enneads,* 4.8,4, quoted in Brown, *Augustine of Hippo*, p. 168.
57. *Confessions*, 2.1.1, p. 25.
58. Brown, *Augustine of Hippo*, p. 169.

human beings to pursue the beauty and wisdom of God. Unfortunately, Adam and Eve chose to disobey God, attempting to be like God. Human beings inherited this biological generation sin – 'original sin became the origin of sin'.[59]

The symbolism of the forbidden fruit in which Augustine tastes his own sin can be contrasted with another garden scene in Book 8 where he experiences conversion. His reading of Cicero's *Hortensius* twelve years earlier has led him to renounce worldly pleasure, and his study of Neoplatonism also enhanced his spiritual aspiration. Augustine writes: 'I stood naked in my own sight and my conscience accused me.'[60] It was 'the habit of the flesh' that held him back. Eventually, reason predominates over his will: 'I could see the austere beauty of Continence, serene and indeed joyous but not evilly, honourably soliciting me to come to her and not linger, stretching forth loving hands to receive and embrace me, hands full of multitudes of good examples.'[61]

Sin occurs when the person misuses his free will. If there is no free will, there is no sin. It is not forced by anything outside, but by a defective operation of the will within the individual: a voluntary movement of one's will from God to the self. Granted by God, free will enables us to live rightly to the extent that it is turned towards God. However, if we abuse this gift of free will, we sin. Thus, free will gives us the power to do good or to do evil. It does not mean the person is autonomous, that he can do anything he desires. On the contrary, it is a freedom given by God to do good and to be free from sin which is a submission to God's will such as Adam and Eve possessed *before the Fall*.[62]

## The Will

When recounting his youth, Augustine focusses on the will and the limitations of human freedom: 'For without Thee, what am I but a guide to my own destruction?'[63] Augustine longs to model himself after

---

59. Lew Ji-Whang, 'Free Will, Self-Consciousness, and the Spiritual Journey of Conversion: St. Augustine and Friedrich Schleiermacher on the Origin of Sin', *Journal of Korean Christian Theology* 25 (2002), pp. 98–99.
60. *Confessions*, 8.7, p. 153.
61. *Confessions*, 8.11.27, p. 158.
62. Lew Ji-Whang, 'Free Will, Self-Consciousness, and Conversion', pp. 97–98.
63. *Confessions*, 4.1.1, p. 55.

Victorinus, who was courageous enough to close down 'his own school of words' rather than God's words. Unfortunately, he writes: 'I was not bound with the iron of another's chain, but by my own iron will. The enemy held my will; and of it he made a chain and bound me.'[64] Locked in bad habits, Augustine's perverted will was transformed into lust; when lust became a difficult habit to break, it became a necessity.

This bad habit becomes a bondage, a chain that binds. Only by turning to God, can a new will be formed. Paul puts it this way: 'You were taught to put away your former way of life, your old self, corrupt and deluded by its lusts, and to be renewed in the spirit of your minds, and to clothe yourselves with the new self, created according to the likeness of God in true righteousness and holiness' (Eph. 4:22-24).

Augustine, however, realises that his old will was deeply rooted, and thus there is a tension between two wills – carnal versus spiritual – which wasted his soul. With God's grace, Augustine finds liberation: 'For I had but to will to go, in order not merely to go but to arrive: I had only to will to go – but to will powerfully and wholly, not to turn and twist a will half-wounded this way and that, with the part that would rise struggling against the part that would keep to the earth.'[65] The approach in which Augustine explores how past habits could trap a person reveals his deep psychological insight into human nature.

Struggling with himself in the garden of Milan after the death of his mother, Monica, Augustine writes: 'You meant to impress upon my memory by this proof how strongly the bond of habit holds the mind even when it no longer feeds upon deception.'[66] Even a bath, which is supposed to relieve the mind of anxiety, does not work. Augustine asserts the past is not past, but is connected to the present. Individuals differ due to their wills being forged by past experiences and habits. The force of habit, however, can only be broken by God. As he writes, 'By your gift I had come totally not to will what I willed but to will what You willed. But where in all that long time was my free will, and from what deep sunken hiding-place was it suddenly summoned forth in the moment in which I bowed my neck to Your easy yoke and my shoulders to Your light burden.'[67]

---

64. *Confessions*, 8.5.10, p. 148.
65. *Confessions*, 8.8.19, p. 154.
66. *Confessions*, 9.12.32, p. 182.
67. *Confessions*, 9.1.1, p. 163.

## Roots of Sin

According to John the Evangelist, 'for all that is in the world – the desire of the flesh, the desire of the eyes, the pride in riches – comes not from the Father but from the world' (1 John 2:6). Thus for Augustine, the roots of sin are: concupiscence (lust), curiosity and pride. In his commentary on *Confessions*, 10.30.41, James O'Donnell writes:

> *Ambitio saeculi* ... defeats humility, the virtue of the self as created being, counterpart of God as creator; *concupiscentia oculorum* seeks illicit knowledge to the detriment of *sapientia*, the authentic knowledge that marks in us the illumination of the divine Word; and *concupiscentia carnis* runs amok in love of created things without reference to God and thus destroys the *caritas* that comes of the Spirit. Thus, even in sin, we reflect the image and likeness of God.[68]

## Concupiscence

'Grant me chastity and continence, but not yet.'[69] The spirit is willing, but the flesh is weak; Augustine prefers to prolong his pleasure in the carnal experience. Continence or self-restraint regarding sex is the beginning of Augustine's conversion as he hears the voice of God calling *Tolle, lege* (take up and read). Augustine is frank about his sexual experience. Bent on pursuing sexual pleasures, he confused lust with love:

> My one delight was to love and to be loved. But in this, I did not keep the measure of mind to mind, which is the luminous line of friendship, but from the muddy concupiscence of the flesh, and the hot imagination of puberty mists steamed up to becloud and darken my heart so that I could not distinguish the white light of love from the fog of lust. Both love and lust boiled within me and swept my youthful immaturity over the precipice of evil desires to leave me half drowned in a whirlpool of abominable sins.[70]

---

68. James O'Donnell, *Confessions*. https://faculty.georgetown.edu/jod/conf/frames10.html. Concupiscence includes not just sex, but also greed, gluttony and vandalism. David F. Kelly, 'Sexuality and Concupiscence in Augustine', *Annual of the Society of Christian Ethics* 3 (1983), p. 92.
69. *Confessions*, 8.7.16, p. 152.
70. *Confessions* 2.2.2, p. 25.

In Augustinian theology, stealing the fruit merely symbolises the subversion of reason, while original sin itself is sexual in nature, the lure of the flesh, as it were. Original sin is spread by sexual desire which weakens the will, but does not destroy it: 'the attendant shame of the concupiscence of the flesh is due ... to Adam's sin'.[71] Further, '*concupiscentia carnis* or *libido carnalis* ... is itself the evil result of original sin'.[72] Thus for Augustine, the sex drive is corrupted because it does not obey the will as the result of Adam's disobedience. Identifying carnal pleasures with the sin of concupiscence, Augustine believes that marriage is good, but virginity for the sake of God is even better.

## Curiosity

Augustine was interested in the theatre, gladiatorial fights and dramas in his youth. These shows were sanctioned by the state, which sponsored the performances that were attended by the public with such intense excitement. In addition, teachers encouraged their students to attend such performances to learn public speaking, thus acquiring eloquence, the art of persuasion and exposition.

Critical of the frenzy and madness generated by the theatre, Augustine also condemns its immoral content. He believes that such performances were bad imitations, encouraging the audience to imitate the pagan gods and heroes. Augustine writes:

> 'Homer invented these stories, ascribing things human to the gods, would that he had brought down things divine to us.' It would have been truer to say that Homer invented them, attributing divinity to the vilest of men, with the result that crimes are held not to be crimes, and those who do commit them are regarded as acting not like abandoned men but like gods from Olympus.[73]

Theatre distorts the minds of people, worshipping villainy rather than worshipping the true God.

---

71. Kelly, 'Sexuality and Concupiscence', p. 88.
72. Kelly, 'Sexuality and Concupiscence', p. 93.
73. *Confessions*, 1.16.25, p. 17.

## Pride

As a child, Augustine acted against the commands of his parents and teachers. When he ignored the good counsel of his mother regarding chastity and laws against stealing, he also rejected legitimate authority ordained by God. Augustine ventured to conform reality to his whims and fancies. Proud and arrogant, desiring to be superior to his friends, he even fabricated stories regarding his sexual conquests:

> I heard them boasting of their exploits, and the viler the exploits the louder the boasting; and I set about the same exploits not only for the pleasure of the act but for the pleasure of boasting … I grew in vice through desire of praise; and when I lacked opportunity to equal others in vice, I invented things I had not done, lest I might be held cowardly for being innocent, or contemptible for being chaste.[74]

In his pursuit of praise for his so-called achievements, Augustine desires to be god-like and denies the goodness of God. Paul says: 'For who sees anything different in you? What do you have that you did not receive? And if you received it, why do you boast as if it were not a gift?' (1 Cor. 4:7). Glorifying himself, Augustine attempts to be like God by praising himself. In fact, pride essentially means trying to take the place of God.

## Manichaean Legacy

As we have seen, Neoplatonism provides Augustine with the idea of spiritual ascent while Paul's teaching leads him to understand sin, grace and redemption by Jesus Christ – they are complementary.[75] The Platonists provide Augustine with a philosophical basis to reject Manichaean dualism. The scriptural authority of Paul's letters to the Romans and Galatians provides theological justification to combat the Manichaean heresy regarding the law, free will and moral responsibility. Paul confirms Augustine's faith in Christianity by his teachings on the dependence of human beings on the creator, their sinful nature and helplessness without the grace of God as revealed in the incarnation and the Trinity, and their need for faith, hope and charity.

---

74. *Confessions*, 2.3.7, p. 28.
75. *Confessions*, 7.21.27, p. 136.

Many of Augustine's works since his conversion to Catholicism have anti-Manichaean nuances. Between 387 and 411, Augustine wrote some fifteen or so anti-Manichaean works. Nonetheless, some critics accused him of being a secret Manichaean when he began his episcopacy, especially regarding his idea on original sin, his teaching on 'two cities', and his notions of sin and sexuality.[76] Perhaps unconsciously, Manichaean concepts spilled over into his teachings and writings. This is not surprising because 'Manichaeism, on both the doctrinal and the practical side, followed like a shadow in the footsteps of orthodox Christianity, which very often could only overcome it by absorbing and making its own some of the fundamental Manichaean conventions.'[77] Thus, one could detect the fear of Manichaeism in most of Augustine's polemical and pastoral writings. It is a legacy that we must acknowledge to understand Augustine of Hippo.

---

76. See Kelly, 'Sexuality and Concupiscence', pp. 81–116.
77. Quoted in Coyle, *Manichaeism and Its Legacy*, p. 328.

# Chapter 2

## *The Divine Comedy*

## Dante Alighieri (1265-1321)

Italian poet, philosopher and political thinker Dante Alighieri is best known for his epic poem, *La Divina Commedia*, *The Divine Comedy* (originally simply called *La Commedia*).[1] An innovation in Italian literature as well as one of the most significant literary accomplishments in medieval Europe, *The Divine Comedy* offers a profound Christian vision of the eternal destiny of human beings. Drawing on his experience of exile from his native city, Florence, Dante offers penetrating accounts of contemporary political, religious and social issues with his wide array of knowledge, stunning symbols and fiery images. By writing this epic poem in the Italian vernacular (Tuscan dialect) rather than Latin, Dante had a profound influence on the development of Western literature to the extent that Italian was the literary language in Europe for several centuries.

In *The Divine Comedy* (1320), Dante utilises both classical and Christian thoughts, combining philosophical and popular ideas of his time to compose his work. Dante begins: 'When I had journeyed half of our life's way' (*Inf.* 1.1), suggesting that the pilgrim has reached middle

---

1. *Commedia* does not mean 'Comedy' as the term is used nowadays but simply a drama or story so structured that it begins in misery and ends in a state of happiness. This chapter is written in collaboration with Denis Chang.

age when he embarks on his journey to the afterlife.[2] Classical poets such as Homer and Horace also start *in media res* (amid things) when commencing an epic. This also alludes to the Old Testament, 'I said: In the noontide of my days I must depart' (Isa. 38:10).

Focussing on *Inferno* (Hell) and *Purgatorio* (Purgatory), the greater part of this chapter discusses Dante's depiction of sin and its purgation, identifying some of the figures he chooses for damnation and salvation and the basis for his choice. Influenced by Aristotle, Augustine, Aquinas and Averroes, Dante is also imaginative in his meditation on the iniquities and failings of humanity.

Born in the thirteenth century, a product of the Middle Ages, Dante nevertheless has a high respect for pagan virtue, although his treatment of 'virtuous pagans' (including Virgil) by placing them together with unbaptised infants in the first circle of *Inferno* called *Limbo* (the realm of natural happiness immediately outside Hell proper) is problematic, especially when his visit to the afterworld is supposed to have taken place long after Christ's death, resurrection and ascension into Heaven. Dante himself does not appear to be entirely happy with the idea of excluding from *Paradiso* (the Heavenly Paradise, featured in the third part of the poem) any virtuous non-Christians, naming only three apparent exceptions (namely, the Roman Emperor Trajan, the Trojan hero Rifeus and Cato), trying in each case to explain the apparent inconsistency.[3]

Always concerned for the welfare and unity of the Church, which to him has both a divine and human face, Dante pulls no punches in his condemnation of simony and all other abuses of ecclesiastical power, spiritual or secular, and anything which has the potential to disfigure the Church as the Bride of Christ.

Popes played a significant role in Dante's life and writings. Deeply involved in the politics of his city, Dante was exiled in 1302 from

---

2. The quotations in this chapter are taken, unless the context otherwise indicates, from Dante Alighieri, *Divine Comedy*, tr. Allen Mandelbaum, https://digitaldante.columbia.edu/dante/divine-comedy/.
3. Dante in Canto XX speaks of an episode illustrating Trajan's concern for justice and mercy. There was a legend that it was through St Gregory the Great's intercession that Trajan posthumously received the faith that saved him. As regards Rifeus, he was, as explained by Dante in Canto XX:1-72, the Trojan hero and character in Virgil's *Aeneid* who was killed defending Troy against the Greeks. Dante places him in the sixth sphere of *Paradiso*, the realm of those who personified justice, explaining that he was converted after being granted a vision of Jesus Christ yet to be born. As for Cato, see below.

Florence at the behest of Pope Boniface VIII (1295-1303). In *Monarchia*, long before the loss to the Church of the papal states in Italy in 1870, he excluded the papacy from temporal powers and possessions. In *The Divine Comedy*, Dante subjected the papacy of his day to thunderous denunciations in *Inferno* 19, *Purgatorio* 32, and *Paradiso* 27. In Canto XIX, Dante consigns Pope Nicholas III to the eighth circle of Hell and makes him announce the imminent arrival in Hell of Pope Boniface VIII and of Pope Clement V (1305-14).[4]

Incidentally, only one pope, apart from St Peter the Apostle, is named as being in *Paradiso*, namely Pope John XXI (1276-77), the only Portuguese pope in the Church's history, learned in mathematics, arts and the sciences (sacred and profane), testifying to the truth that there is no real contradiction between reason and faith.

Although his attacks were directed against abuses of power and not the papacy as such, Dante would never have dreamt that, in 2021, in honour of the seventh centenary of his death, Pope Francis would write an Apostolic Letter[5] to call upon Catholics and non-Catholics alike to read Dante's poem and to 'become his companions', describing him as a 'prophet of hope' and 'a poet of mercy'. Pope Francis was not the only pope in history to praise Dante. Pope Benedict XV, for example, praised the poet in the encyclical *In praeclara symmorum* in 1921 and Paul VI in 1965 made a gift of a gold cross to the City of Ravenna for Dante's tomb on the seventh centenary of his birth.

## Journey to and through *Inferno*

Writing in the first person, Dante starts his allegorical journey as a man who wakes up and finds himself lost in 'a dark forest', having strayed from 'the right path'. The pilgrimage as imagined begins on the night before Good Friday in the year 1300 – with the soul of the Roman poet Virgil (representing reason and wisdom) as his guide when travelling down an inverted cone to the centre of the earth through *ante-inferno* and Hell's nine concentric circles and then upwards out of Hell onto the shores of an island on the other side of the planet where Mount Purgatory with its seven terraces is located.

---

4. George Holmes, 'Dante and the Popes', in Cecil Grayson (ed.), *The World of Dante: Essays on Dante and his times* (Oxford and New York: Clarendon Press, 1980), p. 18.
5. Apostolic Letter, *Candor lucis aeternae*, https://www.vatican.va/content/francesco/en/apost_letters/documents/papa-francesco-lettera-ap_20210325_centenario-dante.html.

# The Divine Comedy

Virgil, who has been sent by the spirit of Dante's beloved Beatrice (who has died young and is already in *Paradiso*[6]), continues to guide Dante through almost of all the realms of Purgatory, at the top of which is the Earthly Paradise (Garden of Eden) before Beatrice herself (representing faith, grace and divine love) arrives to guide Dante deeper into the Earthly Paradise and upwards to and through most of the spheres of the Heavenly Paradise.

Apart from effecting Dante's own personal purification of body and spirit, the allegory represents also a 'universal journey', from recognition of sin and the real possibility of damnation, to the need for penitence and purgation before one can, with God's merciful grace, arrive at the Beatific Vision and eternal bliss of those who are saved on account of Christ's redemptive sacrificial love. Indeed Dante himself states, in his *Epistola a Congrande,* that the purpose is to transport mankind from the state of misery of sin to one of eternal happiness.

Dante's *Inferno* follows the biblical account in the Book of Revelation, which describes the enclosed abyss where Satan resides: 'threw him into the pit, and locked and sealed it over him, so that he would deceive the nations no more until the thousand years were ended. After that, he must be let out for a little while' (Rev. 20:3). The sinners would be punished by being thrown into a lake of fire, described as a second death: 'Then Death and Hades were thrown into the lake of fire. This is the second death, the lake of fire' (Rev. 20:14). Dante also draws from classical sources, such as Virgil's *Aeneid*, for his *Inferno*; for example, there are rivers in Hell: Acheron (*Inferno* 3), Styx (*Inferno* 7), Phlegethon (*Inferno* 7) and Cocytus (*Inferno* 32 to 34). Dante also displays his creative genius when he describes the area outside the river Acheron where the 'neutrals' (i.e. 'the uncommitted') are punished; he calls the area inside the river Acheron Limbo. Dividing Hell into nine concentric circles, Dante describes the punishment of each particular category of sinners with enthralling and vivid images.

---

6. In real life, Dante saw Beatrice Pontinari for the first time when his father took him to the Portinari house in Florence for a May Day party when he was nine and Beatrice eight. He saw her nine years later when she was walking with two companions along a street beside the Arno River in Florence He was smitten by her and wrote about this in his first sonnet in *La Vita Nuova*. He later met her only twice, once at a church and the other at a wedding party. Despite the fact he himself married and had children by another woman and she also married another man, Beatrice was Dante's Beloved but theirs was a spiritual love. Beatrice died at age 24.

During his journey through Hell, Dante, whilst frequently manifesting his sympathy and pity for the plight of particular lost souls, maintains that sin must be punished because it is an offence against God and neighbour. Sin also prevents one from seeing what is true and what is false, and punishment of sin helps restore the balance between good and evil. Following the scholastic tradition, sin for Dante is the misdirection of love, or inordinate love. According to Thomas Aquinas, to choose God is to choose the true good. To choose a creature as an end is to choose what appears to be good, but is in fact evil. Sin is the rejection of the divine good while pursuing some apparent good in creatures. There is thus no middle ground: one must either choose God or be against God. With regard to mortal sin, one chooses life or death. Sin ultimately is the wilful rejection of God, pursuing some other good in place of Him. The human good is to be found in God, thus all our actions must be directed towards Him. Evil lacks this orientation, substituting an alien order for the true good.[7] In other words, sin is a deed or a desire contrary to the eternal law.

Desire includes insufficiency when the she-wolf eats and remains hungry; and as cupidity, the she-wolf is never satisfied, is without peace (*Inf.* 1.58), Dante describes how 'she [the wolf] can never sate her greedy will; when she has fed, she's hungrier than ever' (*Inf.* 1.98-99). In the same way, Augustine asserts that 'for when these [vices] have exhausted the soul and reduced it to a kind of poverty, it easily slides into crimes, in order to remove hindrances too'.[8] Poverty includes hunger that could not be satisfied: 'May you be damned, oh ancient wolf, whose power can claim more prey than all the other beasts – your hungering is deep and never-ending (*Purg.* 20.10-12).

Augustine's understanding of sin has thus made its way to Dante's poem. For example, during their journey to Hell, the pilgrims encounter three fearsome beasts that blocked their way: a leopard, a lion and a she-wolf, which traditionally symbolised lust, pride and avarice, respectively. Its significance includes desire rooted in the flesh or *cupiditas* in the Augustinian sense.[9] In narrating the adulterous affair

---

7. Steven J. Jensen, *Sin: A Thomistic Psychology* (Washington, DC: Catholic University of America Press, 2018), pp. 5 and 7.
8. Augustine, *On Christian Doctrine*, 3.10.16, https://faculty.georgetown.edu/jod/augustine/ddc.html.
9. *The Divine Comedy by Dante Alighieri*, Digital Dante Edition with *Commento Baroliniano*, https://digitaldante.columbia.edu/dante/divine-comedy/.

between Francesca and her brother-in-law, Paulo, Dante examines the psychology of desire in *Inferno* 5. Compelled by love, not controlled by reason, Francesca gave in to Paolo's passion, 'the hellish hurricane, which never rest' (*Inf.* 5.31). The adulterous lovers were tossed in a sea of passion and evil winds. Love, when not controlled by reason, turns into lust: 'they sinned within the flesh, subjecting reason to the rule of lust' (*Inf.* 5.38-39). The lustful are thus the carnal sinners who have lost control of their reason and free will.

## Free Will and Justice

The fourth line of the inscription on the Gate of Hell is 'Justice moved my great maker' (*Giustizia mosse il mio alto fattore*) (*Inf.* 3.4). If there is no justice, then going to Heaven or Hell seems arbitrary. There is a correlation between free will and justice because 'Hell is a non-deterministic and freely chosen state.'[10] Dante's *Divine Comedy* is based on the belief that the individual chooses his or her destination in the afterlife. It is the most important choice a person can make, and the consequences of that choice set in when he or she dies. Before death, we are still free to choose, but once chosen, it is irrevocable. In his emphasis on free will, Dante presents the damned as desiring Hell.

For Augustine, free will or *voluntas* is 'the human *psyche* in its role as a moral agent'.[11] It is not merely a decision-making faculty but forms the basic core of the human person. Man is born with a *voluntas*. Effectively, he is *voluntas* and therefore he cannot disclaim responsibility for his actions, arguing that he did not will them. In other words, if a person does something, he intrinsically wills it. A good man wills what is good, and a bad man wills what is bad. Therefore, it makes no sense to say someone is compelled to will something. For Augustine, all actions are done willingly or unwillingly. An unwilling action is done after a struggle due to external pressure. Every human being makes a decision by virtue of free choice (*liberum arbitrium*). In fact, we all have the power of free choice. We make choices under some kinds of motivations. If we cultivate good habits, we will make a good choice; if we cultivate bad

---

10. Teodolinda Barolini, '*Inferno* 3: Crossings and Commitments', *Commento Baroliniano*, Digital Dante (New York: Columbia University Libraries, 2018), https://digitaldante.columbia.edu/dante/divine-comedy/inferno/inferno-3/introduction.
11. John M. Rist, 'Augustine on Free Will and Predestination', *Journal of Theological Studies* 20, no. 2 (1969), p. 421.

habits, our choices will be bad. Bad choices are still free choices, for which we are personally responsible.[12] In *The Confessions*, Augustine admits that he is consumed by lust, a conflict between his will and his 'members'. Yet, he insists that a person has free choice and is responsible for his deeds.

In *The Divine Comedy*, justice is served with *contrapasso*, a principle ensuring that the punishment is appropriate to the crime committed. For example, the lustful souls suffer violent storms while schismatics' bodies are torn apart, respectively reflecting the uncontrolled passions and divisive nature of the sin. The degree of reward or punishment in Heaven and Hell is taught by Augustine: 'in the first city [Heaven], some will outrank others in bliss, and in the second [Hell], some will have a more tolerable burden of misery than others'.[13] The use of *contrapasso* by Dante reveals the justice and fairness of God. The sinners in Hell are distributed in nine circles, in various degrees of misery, according to the wickedness of their offences.

The literary device of *contrapasso* reinforces the line about Divine Justice quoted above on the sign at the Gate of Hell.[14] Ultimately, the consequence of sin is separation from God, which is a punishment in itself. Following Augustine, Dante's Hell is eternal, unending, a perpetual alienation from the life of God.[15] In *The City of God*, Augustine teaches that justice is a virtue that gives everyone his due. There is no justice when a person deserts the true God. It is unjust for someone to ignore God to serve the wicked. When the soul serves God, it exercises control and reason over the body. Reason subjected to God enables one to govern the passions and check the vices.[16]

From an Aristotelian perspective, Dante views the extreme as vice and moderation as virtue.[17] Thus the virtuous person is neither excessive in possessing nor excessive in spending. The sinners in both categories

---

12. Rist, 'Augustine on Free Will', p. 422.
13. Augustine, *Enchiridion on Faith, Hope, and Love* (Grand Rapids, MI: Generic NL Freebook Publisher, 1999), 29.111.
14. See the fourth line quoted. The final line of the sign reads: 'Abandon all hope, you who enter here' (*Lasciate ogni Speranza, vai ch'entrate*).
15. Augustine, *Enchiridion on Faith, Hope, and Love*, 29.113.
16. Augustine of Hippo, *The City of God*, 19.21, https://www.newadvent.org/fathers/120119.html.
17. Teodolinda Barolini, 'Inferno 7: Aristotle and Wealth, with a Note on Cecco d'Ascoli', *Commento Baroliniano*, Digital Dante (New York: Columbia University Libraries, 2018), https://digitaldante.columbia.edu/dante/divine-comedy/inferno/inferno-7/no. 21.

are at odds with one another: 'So did they move around the sorry circle from left and right to the opposing point; again, again they cried their chant of scorn' (*Inf.* 7.31-33). While virtue is regarded as moderation between two extremities, sin is regarded as the excess of desire, as we shall see in the case of avarice or greed. Moderation, however, is not to be understood as being neutral, neither here nor there, sitting on the fence.

## Cowardice and Avarice

Dante introduces to us the so-called 'neutral angels' in Hell who 'who lived without disgrace and without praise' (*Inf.* 3.36), which reveals how he scorns those creatures who are cowards, 'sitting on the fence', refusing to make a commitment. This moral failure is found in Pope Celestine V (1215-96), who abdicated the papal throne after five months on 13 December 1294. Dante places him at the Gate of Hell for his abdication and cowardice, 'I saw and recognised the shade of him who made, through cowardice, the great refusal' (*Inf.* 3.59-60). Dante regards Pope Celestine's lack of moral courage or administrative skills, and his non-commitment, as a betrayal.

The souls in Hell thus include those who are neither good nor evil, grouped together with 'the coward angels, the company of those who were not rebels nor faithful to their God, but stood apart' (*Inf.* 3.37-9). Located at the threshold of Hell, these selfish souls, like the wicked angels, care only for themselves. Later, the pilgrims' attentions are drawn towards the tonsured sinners, including the cardinals and popes:

> *And I, who felt my heart almost pierced through,*
> *requested: 'Master, show me now what shades*
> *are these and tell me if they all were clerics –*
> *those tonsured ones who circle on our left.'*
>
> *And he [Virgil] to me: 'All these, to left and right*
> *were so squint-eyed of mind in the first life –*
> *no spending that they did was done with measure.*
>
> *Their voices bark this out with clarity*
> *when they have reached the two points of the circle*
> *where their opposing guilts divide their ranks.*
> *These to the left – their heads bereft of hair –*

> were clergymen, and popes and cardinals,
> within whom avarice works its excess.'
>
> (*Inf.* 7.36-48)

Condemning worldliness in the Church, Dante gives a thorough indictment of the greed of self-seeking clerics. It begins with his reflection on the misers and spendthrifts.

In *Inferno* 7, the fourth circle, Dante dwells on avarice and prodigality, the misers and the prodigals, who mismanage their wealth in two different extremes. Lacking in moderation and continence, they are greedy or spendthrift: 'no spending that they did was done with measure' (*Inf.* 7.42). In *Purgatorio* 22, at the fifth storey, the terrace of avarice, Dante also includes prodigality. Going beyond the traditional Christian teaching, which emphasises only avarice, Dante holds prodigality as sin too. According to Aquinas:

> Covetousness [avarice] may be understood in different ways. First, as denoting inordinate desire for riches: and thus it is a special sin. Secondly, as denoting inordinate desire for any temporal good: and thus it is a genus comprising all sins, because every sin includes an inordinate turning to a mutable good … Thirdly, as denoting an inclination of a corrupt nature to desire corruptible goods inordinately: and they say that in this sense covetousness is the root of all sins, comparing it to the root of a tree, which draws its sustenance from earth, just as every sin grows out of the love of temporal things.[18]

Dante stresses self-control, moderation and balance in managing wealth. Caught by extremes in opposite directions, the sinners are divided among misers and prodigals: 'where their opposing guilt divide their ranks' (*Inf.* 7.45). Connected to money management is the practice of usury which the Church considers a sin. Here Dante is critical of the newly rich Christians, the mercantile class, rather than the Jews, who were frequently attacked and discriminated against as moneylenders. Dante focuses on families, such as the Black Guelph, who has 'a yellow purse with azure on it that had the face and manner of a lion', and the Ghibelline family, who possesses a 'purse that was blood red, and it displayed a goose more white than butter' (*Inf.* 17.59-63).

---

18. Thomas Aquinas, *Summa Theologica*, https://www.ccel.org/a/aquinas/summa/FS/FS084.html#FSQ84OUTP1, ST I -II, Q84, A1.

Transcending anti-Semitism, Dante denounces Christian families with their obscene moneybags.

Further down the pit, we meet 'simoniacs' (or simonists), clerics who traded in ecclesiastical office who now suffer the indignity of hell fires. Indicting the Church, Dante discusses the sin of simony, based Acts 8:18-20, when Simon Magnus offers money to Peter to purchase the power of the Holy Spirit,

> *O Simon Magus! O his sad disciples!*
> *Rapacious ones, who take the things of God,*
> *that ought to be the brides of Righteousness,*
> *and make them fornicate for gold and silver!*
> *The time has come to let the trumpet sound*
> *for you; your place is here in this third pouch.*
>
> (*Inf.* 19.1-6)

With striking images, Dante denounces these clerics for their complete betrayal of Christ, going against the very values he died for through love and self-sacrifice. Condemning clerical greed, the politicking of priests and the prostitution of the Church as the bride of Christ, worshipping gold instead of God, Dante writes:

> *You've made yourselves a god of gold and silver;*
> *how are you different from idolaters,*
> *save that they worship one and you a hundred?*
>
> (*Inf.* 19.112-14)

Dante's ferocious attack on the clerics of his day stems from his concern for the true nature of the Church. Those responsible for administering Christ to the people are appropriating the power and authority given to them for their personal ambitions and selfish ends. For Dante, the Church is the continuing presence of Christ in the world. Jesus has entrusted this task to the care of Peter but those who are supposed to continue this line of apostolic descent have betrayed their vocation.[19] The place of priests and primates should be pastoral and not political; their role is in the sacred and not the secular domain. Dante's concern for the unity of the Church and the welfare of Christians leads him to condemn heretical teachings that threaten the unity of the community.

---

19. John Took, 'Ecclesiology on the Edge: Dante and the Church', *Studies in Church History* 48 (2012), p. 69.

## Heresy, Violence and Fraud

There are many kinds of heretical sects in Hell, but Dante highlights the fault of Epicureans. Heresy usually refers to theological or philosophical ideas rejected as false by the Church, but followers of Epicurus are more concerned with sensual pleasures. Hedonistic and concerned only with their present life on earth, these heretics thus reject the eternal life offered by God. Being pleasure-seeking, they are too attached to the world with all its pain and conflicts. Essentially a materialistic philosophy, the rejection of the soul's immortality implies atheism as well. Christianity, on the other hand, maintains that body and soul are united in this life and the next.

Dante describes the punishment of heretics: 'Here are arch-heretics and those who followed them, from every sect; those tombs are much more crowded than you think. Here, like has been ensepulchered with like; some monuments are heated more, some less. And then he turned around and to his right' (*Inf.* 9.127-32). Rejecting the heresy of Epicureanism, Dante further writes: 'Within this region is the cemetery of Epicurus and his followers, all those who say the soul dies with the body' (*Inf.* 10.13-15). These sinners buried in the tomb signify their turning away from the life of the Church. Indeed, heresy does violence to the Church and the people of God.

The sins of violence are divided into three types: violence against God, against oneself and against one's neighbour (*Inf.* 11.31). Violence against self and others includes the abuse of material goods, which need to be protected from human destruction: 'Violent death and painful wounds may be inflicted on one's neighbour; his possessions may suffer ruin, fire, and extortion' (*Inf.* 11.34-36). Virgil discusses the sins of fraud which he divides into two types: 'Now fraud, that eats away at every conscience, is practiced by a man against another who trusts in him, or one who has no trust' (*Inf.* 11.52-54). When fraud is committed against those who have trust in him, it is betrayal. These traitors will be punished eternally. Fraud can be committed in multiple ways in our society, as Dante declares: 'hypocrisy and flattery, sorcerers, and falsifiers, simony, and theft, and barrators and panders and like trash' (*Inf.* 11.58-60).

Dante makes a distinction between sin and vice. For example, murder is a sin while greed and anger are the underlying vices and impulses leading us to sin: 'O blind cupidity and insane anger, which goad us on so much in our short life, then steep us in such grief eternally!' (*Inf.* 12.49-51). The greatest sinners in this circle are the tyrants, despotic rulers who committed violence against the people, killing them and taking their possessions. Dante writes, 'I saw some who were sunk up to their brows, and that huge Centaur said: "These are the tyrants who plunged their hands in blood and plundering"' (*Inf.* 12.103-05). Dante's deliberations on violence and tyranny reveal his concern with political tension and despotism in the Italian city-states.

In *Inferno* 13, Dante meditates on the nature of violence against self, such as suicide or wasting personal resources. The pilgrims enter a dark forest: 'No green leaves in that forest, only black; no branches straight and smooth, but knotted, gnarled; no fruits were there, but briers bearing poison' (*Inf.* 13.4-6). These poisonous plants are the souls of those who have committed suicide – they have been transformed from human to vegetative life. Dante points to the idea that 'the unity of body and soul is indestructible. Selfhood cannot be undone.'[20] Here again, we witness his denunciation of Epicureanism.

These wretched souls appear to be plants, but in substance, they are still humans; their sufferings continue as the selfhood cannot be destroyed. Mythological birds feed on the foliage of these plants, causing immense sufferings: 'then the Harpies, feeding on its leaves, cause pain and for that pain provide a vent' (*Inf.* 13.101-02). Dante thus suggests that the unity of the body and soul is never disrupted. We cannot avoid pain simply by destroying our bodies.

In the Christian understanding of the resurrection, we rise again on the last day, body and soul united, 'the inseparable personhood of soul that is embodied and of body that is ensouled'.[21] Thus after the resurrection, those souls in Paradise are anxious to see their loved ones in person:

> *One and the other choir seemed to me*
> *so quick and keen to say 'Amen' that they*
> *showed clearly how they longed for their dead bodies –*
> *not only for themselves, perhaps, but for*
> *their mothers, fathers, and for others dear*
> *to them before they were eternal flames.*
>
> (*Par.* 14.61-66)

---

20. Teodolinda Barolini, '*Inferno* 13: Non-Dualism: Our Bodies, our Selves', *Commento Baroliniano*, Digital Dante (New York: Columbia University Libraries, 2018), https://digitaldante.columbia.edu/dante/divine-comedy/inferno/inferno-13, no. 5.
21. Barolini, '*Inferno* 13: Non-Dualism', no. 18.

Against the Epicureans, Dante insists that earthly relations are not forgotten but enhanced, and suggests that those who committed suicide will not get their bodies in good form: 'it is not right for any man to have what he himself has cast aside' (*Inf.* 13.105-06). Thus after the Last Judgment, the bodies of those who committed suicide will never be fully integrated; they become corpses hanging from the tree: 'We'll drag our bodies here; they'll hang in this sad wood, each on the stump of its vindictive shade' (*Inf.* 13.106-08). Suicide was considered a virtue in the classical age, but Christianity teaches that it is a sin to take away what belongs to God alone – our own life. Further, according to Dante, we create our own Hell. Sinners who do not repent will be stuck with their sins eternally: 'That which I was in life, I am in death' (*Inf.* 14.51). The prime example of a sinner is Lucifer, who is neither dead nor alive as we shall see.

## Pride and Betrayal

The sight of Lucifer in Hell is grotesque and terrifying. The wings of Lucifer cause Lake Cocytus to freeze while his mouth mangles the damned souls of three traitors, Judas, Brutus and Cassius. His six wings, three faces, and mouth are related to his ability to communicate and his status as one of the angels before his rebellion against God. Lucifer is now condemned to eternal silence. Once a sublime angel, Lucifer is reduced to a monster due to his pride; he has forfeited the good through his own fault.[22]

In *Inferno* 34, the portrayal of Lucifer reflects the Augustinian idea that evil is the absence of God. For Augustine, the wages of sin are alienation and estrangement from God, the source of life. Hell is eternal damnation for the sinner. *Inferno* 34 also alludes to Augustine's anti-Manichaeism, which maintains that evil has no transcendental principle. In other words, God did not create evil. The depiction of Lucifer as the King of Hell reveals that evil signals a deficiency, an absence of good, and a negation of God's love. The freezing cold atmosphere in Hell and Lucifer's three pairs of bat-wings signify the absence of warmth and life: 'three winds made their way out from him – and all Cocytus froze before those winds' (*Inf.* 34.51-52). The three faces of Lucifer is a perversion of the Trinity (*Inf.* 34.38-39).

---

22. Dino S. Cervigni, 'The Muted Self-Referentiality of Dante's Lucifer', *Dante Studies with the Annual Report of the Dante Society* 107, no. 107 (1989), pp. 45–46.

In this episode, Dante reflects on the sins of pride and betrayal and the transformation from good to evil. Once the most beautiful and greatest of the angels, it is Lucifer's pride that led to his fall: 'If he was once as handsome as he now is ugly and, despite that, raised his brows against his Maker, one can understand' (*Inf.* 34.34-36). Further, he is neither dead nor alive: 'I did not die, and I was not alive; think for yourself, if you have any wit, what I became, deprived of life and death' (*Inf.* 34.25-27). Deprivation is the essence of Hell in the Augustinian sense. The fall of Lucifer, however, moves God to provide a remedy for sinful humanity, the creation of Purgatory, 'left here this hollow space and hurried upward' (*Inf.* 34.125).

## *Purgatorio*

The Catholic teaching on purgatory has roots that go back to the pre-Christian Judaic and early Church practice of prayers for the dead as attested to by, among other things, inscriptions on tombs of Christians buried in the catacombs and by the writings of Church Fathers who interpret various passages in Catholic canonical and deuterocanonical books of the Bible in support.[23]

This teaching is associated with the need for purgation inasmuch as 'nothing defiled can enter Heaven' (cf. Rev. 21:27). That is why Dante portrays those being ferried into Purgatory as joyfully singing since they know that they are sure of their final destiny of Heaven after being cleansed in Purgatory. Known as 'the third place', Purgatory is an intermediary in the other world where the dead are purified and helped by the prayers of the living in line with Church doctrine on the Communion of Saints.[24] It also offers sinners (but not those who die in a state of mortal sin) a second chance to enter eternal life.

In his 1984 book '*The Birth of Purgatory*' the late Jacques Le Goff, an agnostic and medievalist of international renown, argues that the conception of purgatory *as a physical place,* rather than as a state, dates to the twelfth century, fuelled by the many medieval otherworld-journey narratives. He observes that it gives the Church including the laity tremendous power over the dead.[25] It sadly has been exploited by

---

23. 2 Macc. 12:41–46 (deuterocanonical), 2 Tim. 1:8, Matt. 12:32; Luke 18:16–19, 23:43; 1 Cor. 3:11–15; Heb. 12:29.
24. Jacques Le Goff, *The Birth of Purgatory* (Chicago: University of Chicago Press, 1983), p. 1.
25. Le Goff, *Birth of Purgatory*, p. 12.

worldly clerics and simonists for financial gain, abuses which Dante roundly condemns without detracting from his faith in the existence of purgatory. Indeed the idea of purgatory has further been enhanced by the poetic genius of Dante himself, as he devotes a third of his epic drama to 'the third place'.

Ingenious and creative, Dante portrays purgatory as a terraced mountain to reflect the experience of its inhabitants based on the seven deadly sins – pride, envy, wrath, sloth, lust, avarice and gluttony. Dante refers to Adam and Eve as the 'first people' on earth: 'Then I turned to the right, setting my mind upon the other pole, and saw four stars not seen before except by the first people' (*Purg*. 1.22-24). Thus Purgatory is where people purge their sins to be like their first parents, in a state of prelapsarian innocence before the Fall.

Dante's Purgatory, in addition to two levels constituting Ante-Purgatory, is comprised of seven circular terraces with diminishing circumferences as one moves to the summit. In each circle, the sinner is purged of one of the seven deadly sins, in turn pride, envy, wrath, sloth, avarice, gluttony and lust. As the souls in Purgatory proceed, they are purged to become purer till they reach Paradise. Purgation occurs in three ways: first, by physical punishment that mortifies the flesh and instils virtues; second, by contemplating the sins to be purged and virtues to be adopted; third, purgation is assisted by the prayers of the living. In their journey upwards, love is the governing principle as the souls progress in their spiritual life because the existence of sin is due to the absence of God's love or the good. Delayed by sin, the soul slowly regains the love of God as it makes its way upwards.[26] It is only at the summit that the genuine love of God is restored.

The inclusion in Purgatory of several people who were excommunicated suggests Dante's independence regarding papal authority. To be excommunicated means to be excluded from the communion of all believers. Regarding the excommunication of Manfredi, Dante writes: 'And if Cosenza's pastor, who was sent to hunt me down – alive or dead – by Clement, had understood this facet of God's mercy' (*Purg*. 3.124-26). In other words, the Pope who excommunicates Manfredi through the Archbishop of Cosenza has not experienced the mercy of God. Manfredi deserves to be in Purgatory because he repented of his sins at the last moment of his life, as did Bonconte da Montefeltro in *Purgatorio* 5. Just

---

26. Le Goff, *Birth of Purgatory*, p. 339.

as a papal absolution alone cannot save you (*Inf.* 27), neither can a papal excommunication irrevocably condemn you.

The sins of those in Dante's Purgatory are not necessarily only venial sins but the same capital sins that land some souls in Hell. The only difference is that the sinners in Purgatory have repented of those sins before death but have not expiated or fully expiated for all their sins. These seven classes of sins are symbolically traced on Dante's forehead by an angel seven times with the letter 'P' (*peccatto*, sin) with the tip of his sword:

> *Upon my forehead, he traced seven P's*
> *with his sword's point and said: 'When you have entered*
> *within, take care to wash away these wounds.'*
> (*Purg.* 9.112-14)

When Dante moves to the next circle or terrace, another angel wipes away one of the Ps engraved on his forehead. Virgil explains that the seven deadly sins are caused by the perversion of love. It is a violation against the love of God, which is transformed into the love of evil, resulting in three kinds of hatred towards neighbour: pride, envy and wrath.

> *Thus, if I have distinguished properly,*
> *ill love must mean to wish one's neighbor ill;*
> *and this love's born in three ways in your clay.*
>
> *There's he who, through abasement of another,*
> *hopes for supremacy; he only longs*
> *to see his neighbor's excellence cast down.*
>
> *Then there is one who, when he is outdone,*
> *fears his own loss of fame, power, honor, favor;*
> *his sadness loves misfortune for his neighbor.*
> (*Purg.* 17.112-23)

Dante describes the seven deadly sins in a hierarchical order, placing pride as the most grievous offence, followed by envy, wrath, avarice, gluttony, sloth and lust. He divides lustful souls into two distinct groups, heterosexuals and homosexuals. Regardless of social and cultural norms, Dante gives homosexuals no less than heterosexuals who repented of their sins before death the benefits of Purgatory (*Purg.*

26.77-78, 79). Seeing sex as an excess of desire, he believes it is the same impulse that causes both heterosexuals and homosexuals to fall.[27] Dante describes desire as the movement of the spirit that can lead us to do good as well as evil: 'so does the soul, when seized, move into longing, a motion of the spirit, never resting' (*Purg.* 18.31-32). Unless guided by reason, desire can lead us astray regardless of a person's sexual orientation (to use a modern term). Dante's understanding of human sexuality is balanced and tolerant in contrast with medieval attitudes and even the mindsets of many people today, although his *Inferno* does have a circle within which 'Sodomites' among others are confined.

Finally, those souls who await the final moment of their life before repenting cannot be admitted into Purgatory without 'good' prayers:

> *And I: 'But if a spirit who awaits*
> *the edge of life before repenting must –*
> *unless good prayers help him – stay below'*
>
> (*Purg.* 11.127-29)

Thus Dante is surprised to see Forese Donati, who was slow to repent, in Purgatory less than five months after his death: 'you come so quickly here? I thought to find you down below, where time must pay for time' (*Purg.* 23.83-84).

## The Case of Cato

Not all who committed suicide are consigned to Hell in Dante's drama. The guardian at the entrance to Purgatory is Cato of Utica, who committed suicide in 46 CE to protest against the dictatorship of Caesar. He is a pagan who sacrificed his life rather than submit to Caesar's authoritarian rule. Placing Cato in Purgatory demonstrates Dante's respect for Cato's sacrifice for the cause of political freedom:

> *Now may it please you to approve his coming;*
> *he goes in search of liberty – so precious,*
> *as he who gives his life for it must know.*

---

27. Teodolinda Barolini, '*Purgatorio* 26: Human Sexuality', *Commento Baroliniano*, Digital Dante (New York: Columbia University Libraries, 2014), https://digitaldante.columbia.edu/dante/divine-comedy/purgatorio/purgatorio-26/paragraph no. 11.

> *You know it – who, in Utica, found death*
> *for freedom was not bitter, when you left*
> *the garb that will be bright on the great day.*
>
> (*Purg.* 70-75)

There is a moral implication for Dante, because the souls in Purgatory work to liberate themselves from the vices that enslave them. Placing a pagan who committed suicide in Purgatory also shows the influence of classical antiquity on Dante's drama. His portrait of Cato was borrowed from Lucan, the ancient Roman poet. The theological implication is that even someone who lived before the birth of Christ can be saved. In other words, Cato has 'implicit faith', as taught by Thomas Aquinas,[28] even though there is reason to question whether Dante is prepared to go as far as Aquinas in his understanding of 'implicit faith'. It is clear, however, that Dante thinks that Cato cannot be held accountable according to the Church's teaching against suicide. There are always, among other things, issues of motivation and of 'culpability' to be resolved before anyone can be justly condemned.

## Dante's Self-Purification and His Three Morning-Dreams in Purgatory

It is in the context of Dante's self-purification that his three morning-dreams in Purgatory should be understood. The first is the Dream of the Eagle and occurs in *Purgatorio* 9. It is highly charged with disorder, violence, masculine eroticism and aggression that includes images of the Rape of Philomela by Tereus in Greek mythology as Dante dreams of being swept upwards by a terrifying golden Eagle. After waking he learns from Virgil that St Lucy has carried him in his dream-state from Ante-Purgatory to the Gate of Purgatory proper, where there are three steps representing the Sacrament of Penance (or Reconciliation) requiring confession, contrition and satisfaction. Dante is shortly afterwards admitted into the first terrace of Purgatory for purgation of the sin of pride.

The second is the Dream of the Siren that occurs in *Purgatorio* 29, on the fourth terrace (sloth or *acedia*) after five cantos dealing chiefly with love and free will. When the woman who becomes the Siren first

---

28. Jason M. Baxter, *A Beginner's Guide to Dante's Divine Comedy* (Grand Rapids, MI: Baker Academic, 2018), p. 84.

appears in the dream, she is an ugly hag but is transformed into a sensual woman of seductive charm who begins to sing (like the Sirens to Ulysses and the crew in Homer's epic poem *Odyssey*) only after Dante has affixed his gaze and projected his desires onto her.

In the midst of the song, a Lady appears and urges Virgil to lay bare the Siren's belly, whereupon a putrid stench is released. It is Dante's recognition that the stench has originated from his own projected desires that leads to his moral awakening. The Lady has been variously interpreted as Beatrice or as Dante's power of choice or free will.[29] The help or grace thus given to Dante to recognise as false his own projected image of what is lovable does not negate free will but strengthens him to make the right choice and so to escape ensnarement.

The third is the Dream of Leah and Rachel which occurs in *Purgatorio* 27 on the seventh terrace (where lust is purged). Dante has by now reached the steps which lead from the seventh terrace to the top of the Mount (the Earthly Paradise) and has fallen asleep just before daybreak.

Unlike his two previous dreams, there is nothing disordered about the third. Dante sees two biblical characters, namely Leah and her younger sister Rachel, in a pastoral setting. Leah was Jacob's first wife and bore him seven children; Rachel was his second wife who died during childbirth (Gen. 29-30 and 35). Leah is conventionally presented as representing the 'active' way of life, gathering flowers and making them into a garland, whereas Rachel represents the 'contemplative', constantly looking at her own reflection in the mirror. They are somewhat like Martha and Mary in the Gospel story except that Martha is busily preparing food for their guest Jesus, and Mary is portrayed as sitting at Jesus' feet and listening attentively to him (Luke 10), looking at his face rather than her own reflection.

## Towards *Paradiso:* From the Earthly to the Heavenly Paradise

The tranquillity and beauty of the third dream serves to whet Dante's appetite for what awaits him inside the Earthly Paradise. Virgil is still Dante's fatherly guide but since leaving the fifth terrace of Purgatory (reserved for the purgation of the avaricious and the prodigal) he has been joined by Statius (an important first-century Latin poet whose

---

29. Tomas Antonio Valle, 'A New Perspective in Dante's Dream of the Siren', *The Oswald Review': An International Journal of Undergraduate Research and Criicism in the Discipline of English* 15 (2013): article 3.

conversion to Christianity is attributed in part to reading Virgil's poems, in particular to Virgil's condemnation of prodigality). They enter the Earthly Paradise only after going through a wall of fire without being harmed.

His mission accomplished, Virgil quietly disappears to return to Limbo almost at the same time as Beatrice arrives at the Earthly Paradise. She is beautiful beyond comparison, seated in a griffin-driven chariot as part of a Holy Pageant and stopping opposite where Dante stands enraptured. Her handmaidens then sprinkle Dante with flowers representing the four cardinal virtues of prudence, justice, fortitude and temperance and the three theological virtues of faith, hope and charity, which are also represented by the white veil, the green robe and a flame-colour dress worn by Beatrice.

Beatrice addresses Dante by name when she tells him not to weep over Virgil's departure (*Purg.* 30.55-57) – the only occasion when the name of 'Dante' is spoken in the drama. She reproves him for inconstancy towards her after her death and for straying from the right path, in effect taking Dante to task for not living up to what he himself had advocated in his youthful work *La Vita Nuova* (1292-93), namely the idea of fidelity to the beloved even after the beloved's demise. She demands, and Dante humbly makes, a full and contrite confession. He later allows himself to be immersed in the water of the river Lethe to purge his memory of sin and, upon reaching the river Eunoe, uses its water to refresh and enhance his memory of all the good he has done or experienced. At this point Statius quietly leaves the scene. Dante is now ready to be taken upwards in Beatrice's company into the Heavenly Paradise.

## Beauty and the Eyes that Reflect the Splendour of God

Beatrice becomes even more beautiful as they ascend through the nine-plus spheres of *Paradiso* and in getting closer to God. As Dante looks into Beatrice's radiant 'emerald' eyes he sees beauty and the light of God reflected in them. At first he has to avert his own eyes from the radiance to avoid being completely overwhelmed, but after a while is able by simply looking into Beatrice's eyes to ascend higher. As the great theologian Hans Urs von Balthasar puts it: 'Beatrice looks up to God, and her eyes mirror Heaven. Dante looks into that mirror and finds himself gradually carried up above.'[30]

---

30. Hans Urs von Balthasar, *The Glory of the Lord: A Theological Aesthetics*, vol. III. *Lay Styles*, tr. Andrew Louth, John Saward, Martin Simon and

Beatrice, however, after taking Dante through almost all the heavenly spheres and explaining to him many mysteries of the cosmos and spiritual truths, turns to Dante with a smile to remind him that not alone in her eyes is Paradise.[31] Beatrice has to yield her place as guide to St Bernard of Clairvaux (1090-1153), an abbot and mystic closely identified with devotion to the Blessed Virgin Mary, the creature closest to God. St Bernard suddenly appears to accompany Dante in the celestial voyage, deeper than where Beatrice has brought him into the Empyrean, the tenth and highest Heaven of pure light and love, to seek her intercession so that he may be vouchsafed a glimpse of the Blessed Trinity surrounded by the nine choirs of the heavenly angelic host[32] and the large assembly of Blessed in Heaven symbolised by the Celestial Rose, the dominant focus of which is the Blessed Virgin herself, all praying and singing hymns of praise, joy and thanksgiving to and in adoration of the triune God who is love itself and in whom beauty, goodness and truth are indivisibly one.

When Dante looks into the Blessed Virgin's glorious eyes, instead of returning his gaze, she looks into the Eternal Light of the Blessed Trinity which is then reflected therein. Dante immediately confesses that not even the eyes of Beatrice pierce with such insight, preparing him for a more direct glimpse of the Beatific Vision. Having seen what he is granted to see, the enlightened and transformed Dante the pilgrim finds himself transported back to Ravenna around midnight of 14 April, a week after leaving it.

## A 'Trinitarian Thinker': Dante's Numerical Symbolism and Architectural Super-Symmetry

Dante thinks in trinitarian terms, with 3s and multiples of 3s in the poem and never forgetting that the number 3 itself is $1 \times 3$ (representing the unity of God in 3 Persons). The poem itself is divided into the three books *Inferno*, *Purgatorio* and *Paradiso*, each of which has 33 cantos

---

Rowan Williams (San Francisco: Ignatius Press, 1986), pp. 31–32, cited by Darrell Falconburg in 'Following the Gaze: Beatrice's Eyes and Beauty in the Divine Comedy', Voegelinview.com.

31. Dante, *Paradiso*, XVII:13–21.
32. The nine orders or choirs of angels: Seraphim, Cherubim, Thrones, Dominions (or 'Dominations'), Virtues, Powers, Principalities, Archangels and Angels, divided into three ranks each comprising three orders. See Thomas Aquinas, *Summa Theologica* (ST I, Q108, A6 and I, Q108, A5).

with one extra canto in the first book to serve as a prologue and with each canto consisting of three-lined stanzas, and with each book ending with the word 'star'.

Hell itself has nine spheres (3×3) although there is an Ante-Hell (which in one interpretation consists of two levels, making eleven which means that it does not possess the perfection of the number ten. Purgatory, apart from having seven terraces, has two levels of Ante-Purgatory (totalling nine), plus the Earthly Paradise at the top, making ten. The height of Mount Purgatory is the same as the depth of Hell.

The Heavenly Paradise is spoken of by reference to nine heavenly but material spheres. These are the spheres of seven 'planets' (with the earth in the centre and with the sun being for this purpose treated like one of the planets), the fixed stars and the Premium Mobile, with the moon being imagined as being the smallest, dimmest and slowest in the speed of its orbit, the larger the sphere the brighter and the faster, and with the Premium Mobile being the largest sphere with the fastest orbit and controlling the other material spheres. The Empyrean is the tenth sphere but it is non-material, thus adding a fourth dimension that is outside time and space. It too has nine spheres with the nine choirs of angels, with the Seraphim in the sphere closest to God in the centre of the Empyrean.

The Celestial Rose is massive, circular, multidimensional and indescribably more radiantly beautiful and intricately structured than any Gothic cathedral with rose windows. It has tier upon tier of petalled rows of seats for the saints of the blessed Assembly, with the Blessed Virgin Mary at its centre as represented in many rose windows. One of the names by which Mary is invoked is the Mystical Rose. The famous stained-glass rose window in the Notre Dame Cathedral of Paris is sometimes used to illustrate the three objective attributes of beauty as defined by Aquinas, namely *integritas* (integrity or wholeness), *consonatia* (proportion) and *claritas* (clarity, effulgence or radiance). The beauty that Dante has seen in the Heavenly Paradise however goes beyond any human conception or experience of beauty. 'Eye hath not seen, nor ear heard, neither have entered into the heart of man, the things which God hath prepared for them that love him' (1 Cor. 2:9-10; King James Version).

## Pagans and Non-Christians: The Emptying of Limbo?

As indicated above, Dante's Limbo (Latin '*limbus*' meaning edge) is located at the edge or first circle of Dante's Hell. It is there that Dante finds unbaptised infants as well as virtuous pagans who lived before Christianity or in places where the Gospel was not preached. They include poets and philosophers from classical antiquity such as Homer, Virgil, Aristotle and Plato, as well as Muslims such as Saladin, Avicenna and Averroes. Theologians imagine Limbo as a privileged state or place where souls are deprived of God's presence but suffer no physical pain, only deprivation: 'The sighs arose from sorrow without torments, out of the crowds – the many multitudes – of infants and of women and of men' (*Inf.* 4.28-30).

Even though Dante's treatment of 'virtuous pagans' is problematic, we can see from the names recorded in *Inferno* 4, which included Jews, Greeks, Romans and Egyptians, that Dante embraces pluralism and multiculturalism. He wonders where justice is if we condemn a good person just because he has no knowledge of Christianity due to cultural or geographical differences:

> *For you would say: 'A man is born along*
> *the shoreline of the Indus River; none*
> *is there to speak or teach or write of Christ.*
> *And he, as far as human reason sees,*
> *in all he seeks and all he does is good:*
> *there is no sin within his life or speech.*
>
> *And that man dies unbaptized, without faith.*
> *Where is this justice then that would condemn him?*
> *Where is his sin if he does not believe?'*
>
> (*Par.* 19.70-78)

One could argue that these sentiments should have led Dante to take the further step of emptying Limbo (which is only a theological hypothesis and has never been defined by the Church as an article of faith), at least after Christ's death, resurrection and ascension into Heaven. According to St Jerome and others (interpreting Eph. 4:8-10, a difficult passage in the Bible which speaks of the Lord descending into the depths of the earth and ascending on high leading 'captivity captive') the risen Lord Jesus took with him the souls in Limbo, and not only the Patriarchs of the Old Testament, into the glory of Heaven.

The sentiments expressed by Dante, pushed to their logical conclusion, would have anticipated Pope Benedict XVI's promulgation in 2007 of a document he signed abolishing the concept of Limbo for unbaptised infants. Those sentiments would also have been consistent with the positive teaching of Vatican II concerning non-Christians and the value of and need for inter-religious dialogue.

Steeped in the classical and Roman-Judaeo traditions, Dante is attached to paganism and Christianity, revealing his spirituality's complexity in *The Divine Comedy*. Although born a Christian, paganism was also part of his *alter ego*, which led his imagination to travel to the other world with Virgil as his guide.[33] We thus have a Christian pilgrim led by a pagan leader, who is also his teacher, master, lord and even father. Rarely in Western literature do we witness such reverence and respect expressed in a relationship between a pagan guardian and his Christian ward in an epic poem. A humanistic scholar far ahead of his times, Dante was a literary genius who gave sublime expression to his exploration of human destiny.

---

33. Kenelm Foster, *The Two Dantes, and Other Studies* (Berkeley, CA: University of California Press, 1977), p. 156.

# Chapter 3

## *Hamlet* and *The Tempest*

### William Shakespeare (1564-1616)

William Shakespeare, possibly the greatest dramatist of all time, was born in Stratford-upon-Avon, Warwickshire, England. A writer of great creative and poetic powers, his plays, written for small local theatres, are now read and performed in many countries. As his contemporary poet and dramatist, Ben Jonson, rightly says, Shakespeare 'was not of an age, but for all time'.[1]

Other writers may be creative and poetic but few could match the way Shakespeare weaves his diction and rhetoric to craft a variety of human situations with memorable images and convincing expressions. His plays command sympathy, elicit emotions and foster psychological participation. His works have been translated into different languages and performed in different cultural contexts far removed from Elizabethan England. In addition to his profound humanistic outlook, Shakespeare's dramas are firmly engrained with biblical and Christian influence.

---

1. Ben Jonson in his poem 'To the Memory of My Beloved, the Author Mr. William Shakespeare'. 'Shakespeare's Genius', *Britannica*, https://www.britannica.com/topic/Shakespeares-Genius-1733556.

A Christian philosopher, Shakespeare is

> certainly not only a thinker and a Godly man in the broadest, truest sense, but a discerner and purveyor of heavenly light, of something far above ecclesiasticism, clericalism, creed, dogma, or doctrine. In his day, the Scriptures had been for the first time, over the objection of the established church, made available to the people. … Shakespeare in fact brought the Bible to the theatre.[2]

In this chapter, we will discuss two plays by Shakespeare: *Hamlet* and *The Tempest*. In *Hamlet*, we examine the tortured personality of Hamlet, the Ghost in relation to his purgatorial status and the conflict of Claudius in the 'Prayer Scene'. With *The Tempest*, we investigate biblical allusions and Christian teaching on repentance, forgiveness, reconciliation and regeneration.

## *The Tragedy of Hamlet*

The play opens with Hamlet mourning his father, who has been killed, and lamenting his mother Gertrude's hasty marriage to his uncle, Claudius, within a month of his father's death. His father's Ghost appears and informs Hamlet that he had been poisoned by Claudius and therefore must be avenged. Hamlet seems doubtful about the Ghost's command, fearing it might be the devil provoking him to commit a heinous crime. Upon further investigation and with more visits from the Ghost, Hamlet decides to carry out the vengeful deed. Hamlet seeks to deceive Claudius and others by pretending to be mad; his melancholic nature makes his feigning believable.

Hamlet's close friend Horatio confirms that Claudius is guilty. In fact, driven by a guilty conscience, Claudius seeks to find out the cause of Hamlet's bizarre behaviour by employing Rosencrantz and Guildenstern, Hamlet's acquaintances, to spy on him. Aware of their conspiracy, Hamlet acts like a lunatic in front of them. The pompous Polonius, an old courtier, thinks that Hamlet is lovesick over his daughter, Ophelia. Despite her sincerity, Hamlet believes that Ophelia is also contriving against him. He treats her harshly, feigning madness.

---

2. Quoted in Grace R. W. Hall, *The Tempest as Mystery Play: Uncovering Religious Sources of Shakespeare's Most Spiritual Work* (Jefferson, NC: McFarland & Co., 1999), p. 5.

To determine the guilt of Claudius, Hamlet arranges the staging of a play, *The Mousetrap* (also known as *The Murder of Gonzago*), with a group of visiting actors, in order to mirror the circumstances of his father's death, as narrated by the Ghost. The play confirms the guilt of Claudius, as revealed by his reaction. Hamlet, convinced of the treachery of Claudius, swiftly confronts his mother in the chamber regarding her relationship with Claudius.

Hearing a male voice behind the curtain, Hamlet stabs the person he assumes to be Claudius. The victim, however, turns out to be Polonius, who was eavesdropping to ascertain Hamlet's mental condition. This killing of Polonius convinces Claudius that his own life is at risk. He thus sends Hamlet to England, accompanied by Rosencrantz and Guildenstern, with a secret order to the King of England to have Hamlet executed. When Hamlet discovers this secret plot, he alters the message so that Rosencrantz and Guildenstern are executed instead.

Upon his return to Denmark, Hamlet discovers that Ophelia is dead. It appears that she had gone mad due to the sudden death of her father, Polonius, and committed suicide. Her brother Laertes seeks to avenge the murder of Polonius through a duel arranged by Claudius.

Carnage follows, with Hamlet dying of a wound inflicted by the sword of Laertes, which had a poisoned tip given to him by Claudius. In the scuffle, Hamlet realises what is happening and forces Laertes to exchange swords with him. With the poisoned sword, Hamlet kills Laertes. Present at the duel, Gertrude unwittingly drinks from the poisonous cup which Claudius places near Hamlet to ensure his death. Before he dies, Hamlet stabs Claudius and forces him to drink the poisoned cup. Having fulfilled his mission to kill a tyrant, before he dies Hamlet entrusts Horatio with the duty of telling his story.

## Character of Hamlet

Hamlet's existence is one of perpetual ambiguities as he struggles with his insecurities. Confronted by his father's Ghost, Hamlet decides to act, but doubts torment him. He understands that his father's spirit cries for revenge, yet when he is alone, he rejects what he witnesses:

> The spirit that I have seen
> May be a devil, and the devil hath power
> T' assume a pleasing shape; yea, and perhaps,
> Out of my weakness and my melancholy,

> *As he is very potent with such spirits,*
> *Abuses me to damn me.*
>
> (2.2.585-90)³

It seems that Hamlet has to make a critical decision in a very difficult situation but lacks a moral compass. His choice would have serious consequences for his people and his kingdom, in which he is the rightful heir. Essentially a relativist, Hamlet vacillates in his decision to act.

According to Aquinas, 'man is principally the mind of man'.⁴ In other words, human beings are rational animals endowed with reason. Hamlet exclaims: 'What a piece of work is a man, how noble in reason' (2.2.298-99). When Polonius urges his son Laertes 'to thine own self be true' (1.3.78), it entails a fidelity to one's selfhood, which is based on reason. But for Hamlet, truth is relative – he says, 'for there is nothing either good or bad but thinking makes it so' (2.2.245-46).

Hamlet also holds that the mind is a prison as the individual is confined to a 'course of thought' (3.3.83). Subjected to bad dreams and hallucinations, 'the very coinage of your brain' (*Hamlet* 3.4.137), Hamlet's thought is controlled by the exigencies of his existence. 'How all occasions do inform against me' (4.4.32). His course of thought is prompted by circumstances; how one thinks will determine who one is. Just as circumstances influence our thinking, our thinking also in turn influences our individuality.⁵

In spite of Hamlet's rather bizarre behaviour, it seems that his intention is not motivated by hatred. According to David Beauregard, Shakespeare portrays Hamlet as a character exhibiting 'virtue ethics' rather than 'duty ethics' which is based on adherence to the law.⁶ Virtue ethics, however, involves acting with good intention, right reason and prudent evaluation of the situation. The Ghost commands Hamlet: 'howsoever thou pursues this act, Taint not thy mind, nor let thy soul

---

3. Quotations from *Hamlet* in this chapter are taken from William Shakespeare, *Hamlet*, annotated by Burton Raffel (New Haven, CT, and London: Yale University Press, 2003).
4. Aquinas, *Summa Theologica*, https://www.ccel.org/a/aquinas/summa/FS/FS029.html#FSQ29OUTP1, ST I-II, Q29, A4.
5. Eric P. Levy, 'The Mind of Man in "Hamlet"', *Renaissance* 54, no. 4 (2002), p. 221.
6. David Beauregard, 'Great Command O'Ersways the Order': Purgatory, Revenge, and Maimed Rites in *Hamlet*', *Religion and the Arts* 11, no. 1 (2007), p. 52.

contrive' (1.5.84-85). Thus Hamlet must carry out the revenge, not driven by hatred but for the sake of justice and the common good.

Tyrannicide, the killing of a tyrant, was encouraged in antiquity. Aristotle asserted that great honour is bestowed on the one who kills a tyrant; for tyranny is an abuse of power and acting against the government's goal of forging the common good. With absolutely no regard for the public interest, the tyrant's purpose is for pleasure and to enrich himself by force or fraud.[7] This applies to Claudius, who admits to fratricide, taking over Gertrude and the throne: 'Of those effects for which I did the murder: My crown, mine own ambition, and my queen' (3.3.54-55). His acknowledgement of his ambition reveals him to be a despot of the worst kind.

If the Ghost is a spirit from Purgatory, his cry for vengeance is morally justifiable. Claudius must be brought to justice since he is a tyrant who seizes the throne illegally. This principle is supported by Aquinas:

> the avenger's intention be directed chiefly to some good, to be obtained by means of the punishment of the person who has sinned (for instance that the sinner may amend, or at least that he may be restrained, and others be not disturbed, that justice may be upheld, and God honoured), then vengeance may be lawful, provided other due circumstances be observed.[8]

Vengeance is, thus, a special virtue if it is performed with the purpose of removing harm or preventing evil. Aquinas also asserts that the avenger must be motivated by charity, not hatred. This is in accord with Hamlet's thought late in the play, to avoid evil by killing Claudius:

> *Does it not, think thee, stand me now upon –*
> *He that hath killed my king and whored my mother,*
> *Popped in between th' election and my hopes,*
> *Thrown out his angle for my proper life,*
> *And with such cozenage – is 't not perfect*
> *conscience*
> *To quit him with this arm? And is 't not to be*
> *damned*

---

7. Nicole M. Coonradt, '"To Be or Not to Be?": Hamlet and Tyrannicide', *Religion and the Arts* 25, no. 3 (2021), pp. 243–44.
8. Aquinas, *Summa Theologica*, ST II-II, Q108, A1.

> To let this canker of our nature come
> In further evil?
>
> (5.2.64-70)

Further, Aquinas describes vengeance as a virtue with two opposing extremes, excess and deficiency:

> Two vices are opposed to vengeance: one by way of excess, namely, the sin of cruelty or brutality, which exceeds the measure in punishing: while the other is a vice by way of deficiency and consists in being remiss in punishing, wherefore it is written (Prov. 13:24): 'He that spareth the rod hateth his son.' But the virtue of vengeance consists in observing the due measure of vengeance with regard to all the circumstances.[9]

In the play, we witness Hamlet wavering between these extremes: he is cruel towards Ophelia, Gertrude and Polonius, but appears to be relatively passive towards Claudius as his mind swings from certainty to scepticism. Only a Ghost from Purgatory can help him resolve his predicament.

Before the Ghost vanishes, he commands Hamlet, 'Do not forget. This visitation …' (3.4.110). Hamlet is 'a fine, pure, noble and highly moral person, but devoid of that emotional strength that characterises a hero, goes to pieces beneath a burden that it neither support nor cast off.'[10] Hamlet is a tragic hero, the embodiment of melancholic humour.

## A Melancholic Mind

Hamlet suffers from a disease known to the Elizabethans as 'melancholy'. It is a mood associated with uncontrolled passion in between bouts of acute depression. The Danish philosopher Søren Kierkegaard (1813-55) speaks of religious melancholy, which has symptoms of faith such as doubt, anguish and exposure to trial and temptation.[11] Regarding

---

9. Aquinas, *Summa Theologica*, ST II-II, Q108, A2.
10. Stephen Greenblatt, *Hamlet in Purgatory* (Princeton, NJ: Princeton University Press, 2013), p. 206.
11. Søren Kierkegaard and Walter Lowrie, *For Self-Examination and Judge for Yourselves! And Three Discourses, 1851* (Princeton, NJ: Princeton University Press, 1944), p. 44.

Hamlet, his soliloquies and speeches reveal a disturbed mind, struggling to ascertain the reality of his father appearing to him as a Ghost. Experiencing terror and anguish, he finds it hard to reconcile the request of the Ghost for vengeance with Christian teaching on forgiveness. This dilemma leads him to meditate on the meaning of human existence. Pulled in two directions, Hamlet struggles between his doubt about the reality of the Ghost's revelation and the duty imposed on him as a son. This conflict and confusion continue in the first three acts of the play.

Deeply aware of his inability to act, Hamlet also suffers from a guilt complex due to his neglect of duty. While conscious of the sinfulness of others as well as his own, Hamlet laments his inaction: 'How weary, stale, flat, and unprofitable / Seem to me all the uses of this world!' (1.2.133). It appears that the melancholic man does not want to forget his sins; he also does not want to remember that his sins are forgiven. Furthermore, Hamlet is obsessed with the sins of his mother and his uncle: 'O, most wicked speed, to post / With such dexterity to incestuous sheets! It is not, nor it cannot come to good. But break, my heart, for I must hold my tongue' (1.2.156-59).

Aware of his hesitation to avenge the injustice done to his father, the conflict he feels within himself regarding his Christian belief and the corruption surrounding him are the cause of Hamlet's melancholic humour. As the play continues, his depression gets worse and worse, to the point where Hamlet contemplates suicide: 'O, that this too, too sullied flesh would melt, / Thaw, and resolve itself into a dew, / Or that the Everlasting had not fixed / His canon 'gainst self-slaughter!' (1.2.129-32). In his soliloquy, 'To be or not to be' (3.1.56), we find him questioning the value of life and the meaning of human existence. At the same time, Hamlet has a deep sense of responsibility towards himself as a human being created in the image of God: 'What a piece of work is a man, how noble in reason, how infinite in faculties, in form and moving how express and admirable; in action how like an angel, in apprehension how like a god' (2.2.298-301).

To Hamlet, human existence involves constantly making moral choices; he cannot observe life merely as a spectator. Kierkegaard asserts that 'pure thinking' is a 'phantom', and the person who merely thinks without acting is like a traitor.[12] There are moments when Hamlet feels he is a traitor and a coward: 'A dull and muddy-mettled rascal' (2.2.551). Unless he makes a leap of faith, he will always be trapped in

---

12. Shaakeh Agajanian, 'Problem of Hamlet: A Christian Existential Analysis', *Religion in Life* 46, no. 2 (1977), p. 219.

his own mind and will never find assurance in his attempt to do God's will. Hamlet makes the final decision only when he conceives of the mousetrap to catch the king. Telling Horatio to observe, he says:

> *Even with the very comment of thy soul*
> *Observe my uncle. If his occulted guilt*
> *Do not itself unkennel in one speech,*
> *It is a damnèd ghost that we have seen,*
> *And my imaginations are as foul*
> *As Vulcan's stithy. Give him heedful note,*
> *For I mine eyes will rivet to his face,*
> *And, after, we will both our judgments join*
> *In censure of his seeming*
>
> (3.2.75-83)

Hamlet struggles with his conscience to make moral choices in a complicated situation. Believing in divine guidance, he says: 'There's a divinity that shapes our ends' (5.2.10); 'There is a special providence in the fall of a sparrow' (5.2.205-06). As a Christian prince, his dilemma can be interpreted as a spiritual problem, a representation of the sinner in his struggle with the forces of evil. In the end, he asks for forgiveness from Laertes: 'Give me your pardon, sir. I have done you wrong' (5.2.211). He forgives his mother too. Convinced of the truth of the Ghost's apparition, his mind is no longer divided. Next, we will discuss the Ghost's appearance from Purgatory. As observed in Dante's *The Divine Comedy*, Catholics believe Purgatory to be an intermediate stage after death.

## The Ghost from Purgatory

Shakespeare makes it clear that the Ghost is not a fantasy but a reality:

> BARNARDO
> *How now, Horatio, you tremble and look pale.*
> *Is not this something more than fantasy?*
> *What think you on 't?*
> HORATIO
> *Before my God, I might not this believe*
> *Without the sensible and true avouch*
> *Of mine own eyes.*
>
> (1.1.53-58)

In spite of the fear that the Ghost arouses, he is portrayed not as an evil spirit but as a murdered victim of Claudius. Killed by his own sibling, the Ghost describes his killing as 'Murther most foul', 'unnatural' (1.5.27-28), a violation of nature. The description of his murder elicits our sympathy, compassion and indignation. The Ghost speaks as he returns from Purgatory,:

> *I am thy father's spirit,*
> *Doomed for a certain term to walk the night*
> *And for the day confined to fast in fires*
> *Till the foul crimes done in my days of nature*
> *Are burnt and purged away.*
>
> (1.5.9-13)

Suffering in Purgatory, Hamlet's departed father is being purified for his sins before his entrance into Paradise. The Ghost laments that being cut off from his natural life by his own brother prevented him from making a good confession and receiving the last sacrament of extreme unction (anointing):

> *Thus was I, sleeping, by a brother's hand*
> *Of life, of crown, of queen at once dispatched,*
> *Cut off, even in the blossoms of my sin,*
> *Unhouseled, disappointed, unaneled,*
> *No reck'ning made, but sent to my account*
> *With all my imperfections on my head*
>
> (1.5.74-79)

Initially, Hamlet fears that the Ghost might be an evil and dishonest Spirit taking advantage of his melancholic state of mind in urging him to perform a heinous crime, a sin that would send him to Hell. Hamlet defers his revenge when he sees Claudius praying. As he meditates on murdering his uncle at this apparently perfect moment he says, 'Now might I do it pat, now he is a-praying' (3.3.72). Why does Hamlet hesitate?

## Prayer Scene

The 'Prayer Scene' in Act 3 is pivotal to the whole play because it provides new insights into the characters of Claudius and Hamlet through their highly ironical soliloquies. In fact, the scene is more significant in what *does not* occur rather than what has, namely, the decisions taken by Claudius and Hamlet. Claudius has a chance to repent but refuses; Hamlet has a chance to kill Claudius but refrains. Shakespeare aims to enhance the dramatic effect by probing deeper into the minds and the motivations of these two protagonists, who oppose each other.[13] The opening lines set the tones and reveal Claudius's state of mind:

> *O, my offense is rank, it smells to heaven;*
> *It hath the primal eldest curse upon 't,*
> *A brother's murder*
>
> (3.3.36-38)

Claudius's remorse and guilt are set within a religious framework. We are reminded of the killing of Abel by his brother Cain in the Old Testament. Aware of his sinfulness, the King seems to be trapped and unwilling to repent:

> *Pray can I not,*
> *Though inclination be as sharp as will.*
> *My stronger guilt defeats my strong intent*
>
> (3.3.38-40)

Acknowledging his villainy, Claudius is 'an instrument of evil, but not the very personification of evil'.[14] In this prayer scene, we witness his predicament and often identify with his struggles:

> *like a man to double business bound,*
> *I stand in pause where I shall first begin*
> *And both neglect*
>
> (3.3.41-43)

Like his nephew, his conscience is torn between inclination and desire, and he admonishes himself for his inaction:

> *What if this cursèd hand*
> *Were thicker than itself with brother's blood?*
> *Is there not rain enough in the sweet heavens*
> *To wash it white as snow?*
>
> (3.3.43-46)

---

13. George C. Bedell, 'Prayer Scene in Hamlet', *Anglican Theological Review* 51, no. 2 (1969), p. 114.
14. Bedell, 'Prayer Scene', pp. 116–17.

Claudius wonders if forgiveness is freely given or if he has to earn it. Is the grace of God good enough to forgive him for killing his own brother?

> *Whereto serves mercy*
> *But to confront the visage of offense?*
> *And what's in prayer but this twofold force,*
> *To be forestalled ere we come to fall,*
> *Or pardoned being down?*
>
> (3.3.46-50)

St Paul says 'where sin increased, grace abounded all the more' (Rom. 5:20), but Claudius doubts and asks: what is the purpose of prayer, to prevent sin or to forgive an offence?

> *Then I'll look up.*
> *My fault is past. But, O, what form of prayer*
> *Can serve my turn? 'Forgive me my foul murder'?*
>
> (3.3.50-52)

Claudius thinks that it is futile to ask for forgiveness:

> *That cannot be, since I am still possessed*
> *Of those effects for which I did the murder:*
> *My crown, mine own ambition, and my queen.*
> *May one be pardoned and retain th' offense?*
>
> (3.3.53-56)

In Christian teaching, the conditions for forgiveness include admitting one's sins, asking for forgiveness, seeking God continually and turning away from sinful behaviour. In other words, forgiveness is given when one is willing to make amends. But Claudius is unable or unwilling to give up his throne and Gertrude. He refuses to repent. Nonetheless, he continues to pray, 'Bow, stubborn knees, and heart with strings of steel / Be soft as sinews of the newborn babe. / All may be well' (3.3.70-72), and then Hamlet steps in:

> *Now might I do it pat, now he is a-praying,*
> *And now I'll do 't.*
>     *And so he goes to heaven,*

> *And so am I revenged. That would be scanned:*
> *A villain kills my father, and for that,*
> *I, his sole son, do this same villain send*
> > *To heaven*
>
> (3.3.73-78)

Here, Hamlet is concerned with the consequences of his present actions as well as the afterlife. Elizabethans believed that a person would be judged after death in the state in which he passes away.[15] Hamlet delays in killing Claudius not because of doubt but to damn his uncle for all eternity:

> *O, this is hire and salary, not revenge.*
> *'A took my father grossly, full of bread,*
> *With all his crimes broad blown, as flush as May;*
> *And how his audit stands who knows save heaven.*
> *But in our circumstance and course of thought*
> *'Tis heavy with him*
>
> (3.3.79-84)

It appears that Hamlet is bent on punishing his uncle, not just in this world but for eternity, and hence delays his vengeance. He believes that a man at prayer may be forgiven and thus enjoy the benefits of Purgatory or even Paradise. He will wait for a more opportune moment:

> *Up, sword, and know thou a more horrid hent.*
> *When he is drunk asleep, or in his rage,*
> *Or in th' incestuous pleasure of his bed;*
> *At game, a-swearing, or about some act*
> *That has no relish of salvation in 't;*
> *Then trip him, that his heels may kick at heaven,*
> *And that his soul may be as damned and black*
> *As hell, whereto it goes*
>
> (3.3.88-95)

Rising from prayer, the King says: 'My words fly up, my thoughts remain below; / Words without thoughts never to heaven go' (3.3.97-98). Prayer not sustained by the will and intention to change for the better

---

15. Bedell, 'Prayer Scene', p. 121.

is ineffectual. This would have been a perfect moment for Hamlet to slay his uncle if he knew the futility of supplication. Just as his father was murdered without the last sacraments, Hamlet would ensure that Claudius would be killed in a state of sin that would land him in Hell. The prayer of Claudius, Hamlet remarks, merely prolongs his miserable days as he would die without the last rites.

## Last Sacraments Denied

*Hamlet* is also a play that emphasises the art of dying well (*ars moriendi*) or being spiritually prepared through the reception of the last rites.[16] The Ghost complains that Claudius not only killed him but also left him to die without the sacraments of penance, anointing (extreme unction) and the eucharist (1.5.77), which is worse than the murder itself. As a result, the Ghost has failed to be reconciled with God and is now trapped in Purgatory.

What is so horrible for the Ghost is that he was not given a chance to confess and repent before his death. This implies that Hamlet must execute his revenge in such a way that Claudius be also deprived of the last rites with 'no relish of salvation in't' (3.3.92) as we have witnessed in the Prayer Scene. Hamlet must attempt not only to kill Claudius but also send him to Hell. By inverting the sacramental function, which is to heal and save the penitent, 'the play's sacramentalism becomes curiously sacrilegious'.[17]

Since the Ghost appears from Purgatory, he has a chance to enter Paradise. Unfortunately, while complaining about how he was killed without the benefits of the last sacraments, he cries for revenge. This is contrary to the Gospel's teaching on forgiveness and reconciliation. In Catholicism, the suffering souls in Purgatory are supposed to be atoning for past sins and require intercession for God's mercy by the living, as they are incapable of praying for themselves in their current state. But the Ghost abuses intercession. He defiles his sojourn in Purgatory as he demands revenge rather than repentance. Instead of relying on God's mercy, he takes justice into his own hands.

It appears that the Ghost and Claudius are profoundly different in character: Old Hamlet was a great king and soldier, while Claudius was

---

16. Jay Zysk, 'In the Name of the Father: Revenge and Unsacramental Death in *Hamlet*', *Christianity and Literature* 66, no. 3 (2017), p. 423.
17. Zysk, 'In the Name of the Father', p. 424.

a murderer and usurper. Yet in some ways, they are alike. As monarchs of Denmark, both are guilty of mismanaging the kingdom. Old Hamlet inhabits a 'prison-house' (1.5.14) where he undergoes purgation of his sins, while Claudius struggles in his conscience to purge his sin of fratricide and regicide. Separated from God, both are in need of reconciliation with their creator. The Ghost in Purgatory has a chance to enter Paradise while Claudius is destined for Hell. Be that as it may, we also need to pay closer attention to the 'foul crimes' (1.5.12) of Old Hamlet to get a sense that something is rotten in the state of Denmark (1.4.90).

The Ghost from Purgatory seeking revenge appears to be highly ironic – a reversal of purgatorial exercise. In Catholic practice, the prayers of the living assist the dead in Purgatory to enter Heaven. Christianity condemns murder and commands forgiveness and reconciliation with one's brother. But in *Hamlet*, it is the soul in Purgatory, the Ghost, who appears to the living, seeking not forgiveness, but vengeance. While the Ghost forgives his wife, Gertrude, for her unfaithfulness, he commands Hamlet to punish Claudius, thus revealing his inability to forgive his brother as demanded by his religion, even in Purgatory.

Old Hamlet is not just the victim of murder; he is also 'a perpetrator of foul crimes', and thus, he is also alienated from God. A vengeful Ghost cannot be assured of salvation. In other words, the Ghost makes no 'purgatorial progress towards reconciliation with God'.[18] In the purgatorial and prayer scenes, we are exposed to the inner conflict of the characters leading to multiple murders. Bent on revenge, against Christ's command to forgive, it appears that Hamlet, as well as the Ghost, is just as depraved as Claudius. Similar themes of betrayal and revenge occur in *The Tempest*, but Prospero, the main protagonist, is magnanimous enough to forgive and to be reconciled with his enemies. He realises that he needs to be merciful if he wants to move on in life.

## *The Tempest*

*The Tempest* starts off with a storm raised by Prospero, who was the rightful Duke of Milan, but ousted by his brother, Antonio, because he was too involved in his studies. He was set adrift in a boat with his three-year-old daughter Miranda and landed on an island inhabited

---

18. Grace Tiffany, '*Hamlet*: Reconciliation and the Just State', *Renascence* 58, no. 2 (2005), p. 118.

by the brutish Caliban and the spirit Ariel. Prospero uses his magic to free Ariel, who was imprisoned by the witch Sycorax, Caliban's mother. When Caliban attempted to rape Miranda, Prospero enslaved him to carry out the menial tasks.

With his magic, Prospero raises the tempest in order to bring to the shore of his island a party of Neapolitans returning to Naples from a wedding in Tunis: King Alonso, his son Ferdinand, his brother Sebastian, and Prospero's brother, Antonio. They are brought to the shore by Ariel. However, Ferdinand is separated, leading others to believe he is drowned. Ariel also helps to thwart a plot by Caliban, who joins forces with Trinculo and Stephano (Alonso's servants) against Prospero.

Appearing as a harpy, Ariel rebukes Alonso and Antonio for their crime against Prospero. As King of Naples and enemy of Prospero, Alonso helped Antonio to usurp Prospero. Alonso believes his son, Ferdinand, is dead because he sinned against Prospero. Convinced that the party has learned their lesson and is repentant, Prospero decides to forgive and reconcile with all as he prepares to return to Milan to reclaim his kingdom.

In the meantime, Ferdinand meets Miranda, and they fall in love at first sight. Prospero watches their courtship with careful attention. Insisting that they preserve chastity before marriage, he welcomes their relationship as a means of reconciling Milan and Naples. Their marriage will unite the two contending kingdoms.

The opening scene of the storm has been interpreted as symbolising Purgatory. It enables the play to move towards the Christian teaching of repentance, forgiveness and reconciliation: 'The greater part of Purgatory is concentrated in the tempest itself at the opening of the play. Having passed through this storm, Everyman has reached the enchanted island, which is no less than a setting for the sacred precinct that marks the end of the soul's quest ... the outskirts of Paradise ... even Caliban is aware of it.'[19] An allegorical reading of *The Tempest* pictures Prospero as God, Ariel as an angel, Caliban as a devil and Miranda as a celestial bride or lady chastity.[20] We shall now look at how Shakespeare draws on Scripture to dramatise Christian virtues.

---

19. Quoted in Herbert R. Coursen, *The Tempest: A Guide to the Play* (Westport, CT: Greenwood Press, 2000), p. 133.
20. Coursen, *The Tempest: A Guide*, p. 135. Cox attempts to rediscover the Christian story within the materialist approach in *The Tempest*. See John D. Cox, 'Recovering Something Christian about "*The Tempest*"', *Christianity and Literature* 50, no. 1 (2000), pp. 31–51.

## Biblical Allusions

In *The Tempest*, we observe Shakespeare drawing on the biblical account of the fall of humankind, the Gospel's teaching on forgiveness as a means of reconciliation, and its emphasis on justice and peace. The storm in the first scene evokes a biblical image and cosmic forces. In the Old Testament, tempests were means to break a person, such as in the story of Job (Job 9:17) or the chastisement of people in the story of the great flood. In the story of Jonah, we read, 'Then the mariners were afraid, and each cried to his god. They threw the cargo that was in the ship into the sea, to lighten it for them. Jonah, meanwhile, had gone down into the hold of the ship and had lain down, and was fast asleep' (Jonah 1:5). In *The Tempest*, all kinds of deities or authorities were invoked to pacify the storm. The Gospel stories also affirm the power of the Master to control the elements: 'They were amazed, saying, "What sort of man is this, that even the winds and the sea obey him?"' (Matt. 8:27). Thus, in the storm's opening scene, Shakespeare dramatically presents the themes of equality, the human dilemma and the servant-master relationship. The plight of human existence is presented powerfully within only 68 short lines. We shall now consider the main characters in the play, beginning with Prospero.

Prospero functions as a magician and schoolmaster to Miranda (1.2.172). He confesses to his daughter that he had neglected his duty as a ruler, 'being transported / And rapt in secret studies' (1.2.76-77). By changing his clothes, Prospero plays different roles – he wears a 'magic garment' (1.2.23), and carries at different times a staff, a book (5.1.54, 57), and a rapier (5.1.84). After the shipwreck, Prospero assures Miranda that the passengers are left unharmed:

> *No harm.*
> *I have done nothing but in care of thee,*
> *Of thee, my dear one, thee, my daughter, who*
> *Art ignorant of what thou art, naught knowing*
> *Of whence I am, nor that I am more better*
> *Than Prospero, master of a full poor cell,*
> *And thy no greater father*
>
> (1.2.15-21)

As Prospero asks Miranda to remove his magician's attire, 'Lend thy hand And pluck my magic garment from me. So / Lie there, my art' (1.2.23-25). He begins to tell her about their past: that he was once a

Duke of Milan, but due to his neglect of duty and his brother's betrayal, he landed on this island. Thus from being a magician, he moves to his role as a father, tutor and former ruler of Milan, symbolised by his disrobing and change of attire.

In fact, as tutor or schoolmaster, Prospero guides Ariel's performance and reminds him of his past enslavement by the witch, Sycorax, 'Hast thou, spirit, / Performed to point the tempest that I bade thee?' (1.2.194) and 'I must / Once in a month recount what thou hast been, Which thou forget'st' (1.2.261-63). Prospero also teaches Caliban language, and to name the lights, and punishes him when he misbehaves. Ferdinand is taught restraint, respect and responsibility. Miranda, however, is his primary concern as a father – through Prospero's tutelage, she has become a sensitive and compassionate person. She pleads with her father to show mercy to his enemies.

Prospero, as a schoolmaster, alludes to Moses in the Old Testament, who is a teacher and lawgiver among the Jews, prefiguring Christ, who teaches his disciples to forgive their enemies. Prospero is portrayed like Moses, who carried a staff and the book of law to fight against Pharoah.[21] We see Prospero, wearing a magician's hat, performing his part like Moses delivering the Israelites from the Egyptians. Admitting that the power of Prospero is superior, Caliban says, 'His art is of such power / It would control my dam's god, Setebos, / And make a vassal of him' (1.2.373-75). Setebos is the god of Caliban's mother, the witch, Sycorax. Miranda calls Caliban, 'a vile race' that had 'that in 't which good natures / Could not abide to be with' (1.2.360-61). Prospero can be read as representing Moses, Caliban and Sycorax the Egyptians.[22] This interpretation is evidenced when Caliban curses: 'The red plague rid you' (1.2.365). We remember the last plague inflicted by Moses, resulting in the death of the first-born Egyptians.

Prospero describes Caliban as 'thou earth', 'tortoise', 'poisonous slave', 'hag seed', 'born devil' and 'a thing of darkness'. In the eyes of Miranda, he is an 'abhorred slave' while Trinculo calls him 'a most ridiculous monster' and a 'deboshed fish'. Incapable of human education, Caliban represents the bestiality in human beings. Essentially an 'earthly

---

21. Hall, *The Tempest as Mystery Play*, pp. 55–56. See also David V. Urban, 'Prospero, the Divine Shepherd, and Providence: Psalm 23 as a Rubric for Alonso's Redemptive Progress and the Providential Workings of Prospero's Spiritual Restoration in Shakespeare's *The Tempest*', *Religions* 10, no. 8 (2019), pp. 1–16.
22. Hall, *The Tempest as Mystery Play*, p. 57.

creature', Caliban is pivotal to the play as he points out the 'different criteria of two worlds'.[23] In his brutishness he also represents the noble savage with an unspoilt nature and exposure to civilisation's corruption. St John writes, 'The one who comes from above is above all; the one who is of the earth belongs to the earth and speaks about earthly things. The one who comes from heaven is above all' (John 31:1). This reminds us of Caliban, who is earthly, and Ariel, who is spirit.

Ariel is characterised as 'a symbol of the imagination', 'the spirit of a sensible soul' or Shakespeare's 'art'.[24] A servant of Prospero, Ariel is associated with the messenger of God expressed in Psalm 104:4: 'you make the winds your messengers, fire and flame your ministers'. As 'the spirit of the law', Ariel serves Prospero by revealing the iniquities of Alonso, Antonio and Sebastian: 'You are three men of sin, whom Destiny, / That hath to instrument this lower world' (3.3.53-54). Exposing sin, raising the alarm and tempest, he does not actually hurt anyone, 'not so much perdition as an hair, / Betid to any creature in the vessel' (1.2. 30-31) and 'Not a hair perished' (1.2.217). Appearing as a harpy, he is the minister of Prospero who directs, prevents, blesses and curses.[25] Like the Word, Ariel 'is able to judge the thoughts and intentions of the heart' (Heb. 4:12). Ariel's words move Prospero and help him make the decision to forgive.

## The Forgiveness of Sin

One of the major themes in *The Tempest* is the forgiveness of sin. The main beneficiary is Alonso, King of Naples, that 'inveterate' enemy (1.2.122) who plots with the 'perfidious' (1.2.68) Antonio to usurp Prospero, his brother. Having confronted his enemies with 'torments, troubles', punishing them with 'pinches', 'cramps' (4.1.260) and 'convulsions' (4.1. 259 ), Prospero relents: 'They being penitent, / The sole drift of my purpose doth extend / Not a frown further' (5.1.28-30). Looking at the majestic Prospero and feeling remorse for his sin, Alonso makes amends (5.1.115) and acknowledging his trespass, declares: 'Thy dukedom I resign, and do entreat / Thou pardon me my wrongs' (5.1.118-19). Discovering that Ferdinand is alive through the grace of Miranda, Alonso also seeks her forgiveness (5.1.199).

---

23. Hall, *The Tempest as Mystery Play*, p. 67.
24. Hall, *The Tempest as Mystery Play*, p. 65.
25. Hall, *The Tempest as Mystery Play*, p. 66.

Forgiven by Prospero, 'Go, sirrah, to my cell. / Take with you your companions. As you look / To have my pardon, trim it handsomely' (5.1. 292-94), Caliban responds graciously and wisely, 'Ay, that I will, and I'll be wise hereafter / And seek for grace. What a thrice-double ass / Was I to take this drunkard for a god, / And worship this dull fool!' (5.1. 295-98). Here we witness Caliban coming to his senses, arriving at a 'reasonable shore' (5.1.81), when he realises that Stephano and Trinculo are far below the status and power of Prospero – 'How fine my master is! I am afraid he will chastise me' (5.1.262-63).

Salvation arrives when one realises one's sinfulness, as Ariel asserts: 'nothing but heart's sorrow / And a clear life ensuing' (3.3. 81-82). Of the 'three men of sin' (3.3.53), only Alonso is truly contrite and willing to make amends. Antonio and Sebastian, unrepentant, are 'worse than devils' (3.3.36). Nonetheless, Prospero says, 'For you, most wicked sir, whom to call brother / Would even infect my mouth, I do forgive / Thy rankest fault, all of them' (5.1.130-32). Forgiveness may be given, but it may not be received. Antonio and Sebastian standing aloof in silence cannot hope to receive 'a second life' (5.1.195) given to Ferdinand.

In the Epilogue (6-20) of *The Tempest*, as Prospero prepares to be restored to his dukedom in Milan, he announces to his audience that he will relinquish his magical power to control nature and others and forgive those who have offended him:

> *Since I have my dukedom got*
> *And pardoned the deceiver, dwell*
> *In this bare island by your spell,*
> *But release me from my bands*
> *With the help of your good hands.*
> *Gentle breath of yours my sails*
> *Must fill, or else my project fails,*
> *Which was to please. Now I want*
> *Spirits to enforce, art to enchant,*
> *And my ending is despair,*
> *Unless I be relieved by prayer,*
> *Which pierces so that it assaults*
> *Mercy itself, and frees all faults.*
> *As you from crimes would pardoned be,*
> *Let your indulgence set me free.*

Prospero has thoughts of vengeance but realises that virtue lies in forgiveness. Jeevan Gurung argues that, by forgiving his enemies, he makes them forever grateful to him and thus under his control. Forgiveness is supposed to be a private affair, but Prospero transforms it into a public performance, a political act.[26] Be that as it may, now that he is without magical power, Prospero presents himself as being vulnerable but with the strength to forgive those who have caused him much harm and suffering.

As St Paul says, 'For when I am weak, then I am strong' (2 Cor. 12:10). Without his magical power Prospero might end in despair, unless relieved by prayer. The power of prayer can provide him with the grace to be merciful and pardon those who have sinned against him. Buried in books and the study of magic, Prospero needs to be pardoned for his neglect of his dukedom. The request for prayers by Prospero reminds us of the purgatorial suffering and 'charitable prayer' (*Hamlet*, 5.1.214) for Ophelia.[27]

The allusion to the Lord's Prayer calls for mutual forgiveness, while references to despair, mercy and prayer resonate powerfully with theology, shedding light on the relationship between Christianity and literature.[28] *The Tempest* is also an 'eschatological drama' that points to the coming of God's Kingdom.[29] The play's happy ending fulfils the petition of the Lord's Prayer, 'Thy will be done, on earth as it is in heaven.' Eschatology is concerned with the theme of resurrection.

## Resurrection

The motif of the resurrection from the dead is inherent in *The Tempest*. Swiss theologian Hans Urs von Balthasar aptly asserts that Shakespeare 'takes the risk of portraying the return from the realm of the dead as a pure gift to those in mourning. In these self-contained [romances] the Christian resurrection from the dead becomes the reappearance

---

26. Caliban has been converted or tamed by Prospero's forgiveness. 'Under the pretext of Christian piety, the colonial project is only strengthened.' See Jeevan Gurung, 'Coercion and Conversion Using Christian Magnanimity in Shakespeare's The Tempest', *Papers on Language and Literature* 55, no. 4 (2019), pp. 360–62.
27. David N. Beauregard, 'New Light on Shakespeare's Catholicism: Prospero's Epilogue in *The Tempest*', *Renascence* 49, no. 3 (1997), p. 167.
28. Vittorio Montemaggi, 'Love, Forgiveness, and Meaning: On the Relationship between Theological and Literal Reflection', *Religion and Literature* 41, no. 2 (2009), p. 83.
29. Nancy C. Goodley, 'Thy Kingdom Come: The Eschatological Vision of The Tempest', *Religion in Life* 45, no. 2 (1976), p. 245.

of those believed dead.'[30] Characters assumed to be dead reappear, as we have observed in *The Tempest*. This idea of the resurrection has its roots in classical Greek literature portrayed in recognition scenes where characters separated by shipwreck or abduction found each other in a happy reunion. When the characters reunite, they initially think the person who disappeared has died and been resurrected. Shakespeare draws on this classical concept of recognition in literature and incorporates the Christian belief of the resurrection to dramatise the message of hope, forgiveness and new life with great effect on stage.

With a Christian backdrop, the characters in *The Tempest* are Catholics from Naples and Milan landed on an island somewhere in the Mediterranean. Framed in Christian piety, the sailors cry, 'All lost! To prayers, to prayers! All lost!' (1.1.50). In the closing scene, Prospero says, 'And my ending is despair, / Unless I be relieved by prayer' (Epilogue 15-16). Alonso earlier laments that only a contrite and sorrowful heart would save them from the lingering perdition of divine judgment (3.3.77, 81-82).

Shakespeare also draws on classical and pagan sources in his play when he describes the Europeans landing on an island inhabited by the sorcerer Sycorax, and her god, Setebos (1.2.374), who was worshipped by South American natives.[31] Prospero's use of magic also undermines his Christian belief. Thus Greek and pagan beliefs penetrate and harmonise with the Christian framework of Shakespeare's plays. This fusion of Hellenism and paganism is found in Prospero's farewell speech, which some have interpreted as Shakespeare's retirement from the stage:

> *Our revels now are ended. These our actors,*
> *As I foretold you, were all spirits and*
> *Are melted into air, into thin air;*
> *And – like the baseless fabric of this vision –*
> *The cloud-capped towers, the gorgeous palaces.*
>
> *The solemn temples, the great globe itself,*
> *Yea, all which it inherit, shall dissolve.*
> *And, like this insubstantial pageant faded,*
> *Leave not a rack behind. We are such stuff*
> *As dreams are made on, and our little life*

---

30. Quoted in Sean Benson, 'The Resurrection of the Dead in *The Winter's Tale* and *The Tempest*', *Renascence* 61, no. 1 (2008), p. 3.
31. Benson, 'Resurrection of the Dead', p. 13.

> *Is rounded with a sleep. Sir, I am vexed.*
>
> (4.1.148-58)

In this passage, Prospero reminds himself of his own mortality and the judgment he will face when he dies.

After renouncing his magical power, Prospero appears to the shipwrecked victims in order to unite the living and those presumed dead, drawing on the recognition and resurrection motif when he encounters Alonso:

> *Behold, sir King,*
> *The wronged Duke of Milan, Prospero!*
> *For more assurance that a living prince*
> *Does now speak to thee, I embrace thy body,*
> *And to thee and thy company I bid*
> *A hearty welcome.*
>
> (5.1.106-11)

Prospero assures Alonso that he is still alive. These lines suggest the possibility of a resurrection for all human beings.[32] Believing that Prospero has been dead, Alonso stands in amazement, then repents and seeks forgiveness:

> *Whe'er thou be'st he or no,*
> *Or some enchanted trifle to abuse me.*
> *(As late I have been), I not know. Thy pulse*
> *Beats as of flesh and blood; and, since I saw thee,*
> *Th' affliction of my mind amends*
> *… … … … … … … … … … … … … . .*
> *Thy dukedom I resign, and do entreat*
> *Thou pardon me my wrongs.*
>
> (5.1.111-18)

This resurrection theme is present when Alonso, who discovers his son, Ferdinand, whom he feared drowned (3.3.8), is still alive. He asks Miranda, his future daughter-in-law, for forgiveness. Reconciliation between the two families is made possible by a series of 'quasi resurrections' that Shakespeare incorporates in the various recognition

---

32. Benson, 'Resurrection of the Dead', p. 17.

scenes.[33] Drawing on the Christian belief in the resurrection, Shakespeare broaches the desire of human beings for immortality and to be in reconciliation with each other. In *The Tempest*, Shakespeare dramatises a moral and spiritual lesson on repentance, reconciliation and regeneration.

## Johannine Perspective

In John's Gospel, Jesus performs miracles which enable the disciples to see his glory. Later, we witness Jesus being betrayed, rejected and left to die on the cross. While assuming that he is dead and gone, his disciples meet and recognise him. Jesus imparts in them his Spirit so that they are empowered to forgive sins, as he is now the Lord of us all. He is also speaking to us, his followers, as we read the Scripture: 'Have you believed because you have seen me? Blessed are those who have not seen and yet have come to believe' (John 20:29). These scenes remind us of Prospero who has been betrayed, rejected and cast upon the sea to die with his daughter, and later appears to his enemies, resurrected as it were. In the Epilogue, he calls upon his audience to forgive him just as he has forgiven his enemies. Here we are asked to pray for Prospero as he embarks on his next stage of life beyond the island.

In this reading, we witness a 'recapitulation' in Christ of the reality of the human experience of despair and hope.[34] As we have seen, in *Hamlet* and *The Tempest*, Shakespeare utilises biblical imagery, characterisation, and gospel values such as forgiveness and reconciliation. The text and context of Shakespeare's dramas are essentially Christian in their outlook. Disregarding ecclesiastical control, Shakespeare, in fact, brought the Scripture to the stage.

---

33. Benson, 'Resurrection of the Dead', p. 18.
34. Paul S. Fiddes, 'Story and Possibility: Reflections on the Last Scenes of the Fourth Gospel and Shakespeare's *The Tempest*', in Gerhard Sauter and John Barton (eds.), *Revelation and Story: Narrative Theology and the Centrality of Story* (Aldershot: Ashgate, 2000), p. 30.

# Chapter 4

# *Paradise Lost*

## John Milton (1608-1674)

John Milton, considered the most important English author after William Shakespeare, was born in London, England. His magisterial work, *Paradise Lost*, is perhaps the greatest epic poem in the English language. His theology emphasises freedom of conscience, the importance of Scripture in guiding our faith and religious tolerance. Milton was educated at Christ's College, Cambridge, in 1625, and awarded the Bachelor of Arts (1629) and Master of Arts (1632). Disaffection with the Church of England discouraged him from entering the ministry. While visiting Italy in 1638, Milton met with Galileo, the astronomer, the only contemporary whose name appears in *Paradise Lost*. This classic tells the biblical tale of the Fall of Man. Milton's preoccupation with the question of evil led him to choose the Fall as the subject of his epic poem. Recognising the theological possibility of using a literary form to discuss theodicy, he chose the poetic medium to convey his message.[1]

This chapter attempts to give a synopsis of the Fall and identify Augustine's influence on Milton's theological outlook, focusing on Satan, sin, the role of reason and free will. It concludes with a discussion on *Paradise Lost* as a literary myth. Milton was the first English poet to adapt the literary techniques of *The Divine Comedy* in *Paradise Lost*.

---

1. Anthony C. Yu, 'Milton's Epic Motives: On the Formative Principles of Paradise Lost as Poetic Theodicy', *Criterion* 8 (Spring 1969), p. 26.

Although he was a staunch Protestant, he had read Dante's work with sympathy.[2] We find echoes, allusions and parallels that testify to the importance of the *Commedia* in the *Paradise Lost* narrative.

## Epic Poem

First published in 1667, this epic poem consists of twelve books and almost 11,000 lines, in which Milton adapted the classical epic tradition of Homer's *The Iliad* and *The Odyssey* and Virgil's *The Aeneid*. Focussing on the subjects of war, love and heroism, Milton narrates how the good angel defeats the evil angels, resulting in the latter being expelled from heaven. The sacrificial love of Jesus Christ is contrasted with the conceitedness of classical heroes. Like many classical epics, *Paradise Lost* invokes the Muse, similar to the Spirit that led Moses in the Old Testament. It also begins *in medias res*, recounting the aftermath of the battle in heaven, as detailed in Book VI.

*Paradise Lost* is about the downfall of Adam and Eve as well as the conflict between Satan and Jesus, the Son of God. In this biblical epic which challenges classical heroism, Milton portrays the Son, notwithstanding his victory over Satan, as meek and humble, willing to sacrifice himself for the sake of humankind. The main thesis of the poem expounds how the mission of the Son justifies the ways of God to men. In spite of Satan's success in seducing Adam and Eve, there is always hope for salvation provided by the Son's sacrificial love. This hope enables us to participate in the redemptive act of Christ, now and in the eternal future.[3]

## Fortunate Fall

The story of the Fall of humankind has been told in the Bible, in the book of Genesis. However, Milton is not merely retelling the Scripture. His epic poem is crafted with great ingenuity and creativity, with details of the cycle of events, from the Fall of the rebellious angels to the end of human history, focussing with great psychological insights

---

2. Irene Samuel, *Dante and Milton: The Commedia and Paradise Lost* (Ithaca, NY: Cornell University Press, 1966), p. 45. See also Robert Hollander, 'Milton's Elusive Response to Dante's Comedy in *Paradise Lost*', *Milton Quarterly* 45, no. 1 (2011), pp. 1–24.
3. A. C. Labriola, 'John Milton', *Encyclopedia Britannica*, 5 December 2021, https://www.britannica.com/biography/John-Milton.

on the relationship between Adam and Eve, Satan's deceit and the circumstances and consequences of their disobedience. Drawing on Scripture and the classics, with poetic imagination, Milton's epic poem is divinely inspired:

> *And chiefly thou O Spirit, that dost prefer*
> *Before all temples the upright heart and pure,*
> *Instruct me, for thou know'st; thou from the first*
> *Wast present, and with mighty wings outspread*
> *Dove-like sat'st brooding on the vast abyss*
> *And mad'st it pregnant: what in me is dark*
> *Illumine, what is low raise and support;*
> *That to the height of this great argument*
> *I may assert eternal providence,*
> *And justify the ways of God to men*
>
> (*PL* I.17-26)[4]

Milton presents the speeches of Satan, Beelzebub, Moloch, Belial and Mammon, displaying their rhetorical skills with a variety of persuasive strategies to convince others. With great efforts, the devils seek to present evil as good, making the 'worse appear / The better reason' (*PL* II.113-14). The 'great consult' of the demons concluded with the decision to avoid open war and to explore the possibilities of corrupting God's newest creation – humankind: 'Seduce them to our party, that their God / May prove their foe, and with repenting hand / Abolish his own works' (*PL* II.368-70). Announcing 'deliverance for us all' (*PL* II.465), Satan accepts to undertake this dangerous enterprise to ensnare humankind.

Disguised as 'a stripling cherub' (*PL* III.636), Satan makes his way towards the Garden of Eden. He meets Uriel to inquire about the direction of Adam's abode, pretending that he intends to admire and praise God's work. Deceived by Satan, Uriel replies: 'Fair angel, thy desire which tends to know / The works of God, thereby to glorify / The

---

4. The quotations in this chapter are taken from John Milton, *Paradise Lost*, introduced by Philip Pullman (Oxford: Oxford University Press, 2005), https://search-ebscohost- com.easyaccess2.lib.cuhk.edu.hk/ login.aspx?direct=true& db=nlebk&AN=205554&site=ehost-live&scope=site. Justifying the ways of God to men is synonymous with theodicy. See Dennis Richard Danielson, 'The Contexts of Milton's Theodicy', *Milton's Good God: A Study in Literary Theodicy* (Cambridge: Cambridge University Press, 1982), p. 2.

great work-master, leads to no excess / That reaches blame, but rather merits praise' (*PL* III.694-97). Here we witness Satan's hypocrisy at work and his next victim is Eve, our credulous mother.

Satan journeys towards Eden by carrying 'hell within him' (*PL* IV.20). His tortured soliloquy reveals his anger, frustrations and contradictions: 'Farewell remorse: all good to me is lost; / Evil be thou my good' (*PL* IV.109-10). Satan's speech discloses his emotional entanglement of despair, guilt and suffering. He has been transformed from a magnificent angel to a peeping tom disguised as a toad as he spies on the loving couple with the intention to harm them. In contrast to the hideousness of Satan, Milton describes the prelapsarian couple as possessing beauty, human dignity and innocence:

> *Two of far nobler shape erect and tall,*
> *Godlike erect, with native honour clad*
> *In naked majesty seemed lords of all,*
> *And worthy seemed, for in their looks divine*
> *The image of their glorious maker shone,*
> *Truth, wisdom, sanctitude severe and pure,*
> *Severe but in true filial freedom placed.*
>
> (*PL* IV.288-94)

In their nakedness, Milton emphasises the lack of any sense of shame in human sexuality before the Fall. He is determined to demonstrate that innocent sexuality is different from mere lust.

Milton's view of sex and marriage is deeply influenced by puritan tradition, including a repressive attitude towards women. In other words, women are perceived to be naturally inferior to men. However, Milton's position regarding this issue is not consistent. In fact, his attitude towards women and sex is fraught with contradictions that he never entirely resolves.[5]

God sends Raphael to warn Adam of Satan's plot, 'Lest wilfully transgressing he pretend / Surprisal, unadmonished, unforewarned' (*PL* V.244-45). Thus the punishment for transgressing is severe because of Raphael's warning, justifying the ways of God to men. The encounter

---

5. David Aers and Bob Hodge, '"Rational Burning": Milton on Sex and Marriage', in William Zunder (ed.), *Paradise Lost: John Milton* (New York: St Martin's Press, 1999), pp. 67–87. See also James Turner, *One Flesh: Paradisal Marriage and Sexual Relations in the Age of Milton* (Oxford: Clarendon Press, 1987).

between Raphael and Adam reveals the hierarchy in ranks – Archangel, Man, and Woman. In Books V and VI, Raphael reports on the war in Heaven, the battle between the loyal and rebellious angels; armed conflicts, courageous deeds, spectacular warfare, attacks, advances, retreats and injuries are described in great detail with military precision.

Finally, God sends his Son to drive the renegades to the place prepared for them and then to return triumphantly to sit at the Father's right hand. Concluding this episode with a serious warning to Adam against the sin of rebellion, Raphael says: 'Thus measuring things in heaven by things on earth / At thy request, and that thou mayst beware / By what is past, to thee I have revealed / What might have else to human race been hid' (*PL* VI.893-96). Perhaps this is the only way humans can understand the gravity of disobedience to God. When Adam inquires about the heavenly motions in Book VII, he is advised to seek more worthy knowledge and to contend with his life. Adam then gives Raphael an account of his creation since the archangel was absent during this.

This brings us to the question of Adam requesting a mate from God and his first encounter with Eve, created for the purpose 'of nuptial sanctity and marriage rites' (*PL* VIII.487). Overwhelmed by feminine charm, foreshadowing of his Fall, Adam tells Raphael: 'All higher knowledge in her presence falls / Degraded, wisdom in discourse with her / Loses discountenanced, and like folly shows' (*PL* VIII.551-53). Alarmed, Raphael warns Adam not to let his sexual passion subdue his reason: 'In loving thou dost well, in passion not' (*PL* VIII.588). In spite of Raphael's counsel and Adam's conviction regarding the decency of his union with Eve, love turns to lust after the Fall.

The sense of doom is clearly depicted in Book IX, arguably the best in *Paradise Lost*. Disguised as a serpent, Satan begins to tempt Eve, leading her to request dividing their work so that she can labour apart from Adam in the Garden. Here, Eve is portrayed as overzealous in pursuing her work to prove herself. Her good intention is marred by poor judgement. This separation scene shows how our innocent interests can lead to pride and sin.

In this scene, Eve's mistake is a warning against the danger of placing too much emphasis on work and efficiency: 'Good Works opposed to Christ or his satisfaction, merit, righteousness, mercy, or free-grace in the matter of Justification or Salvation, are not good works, but proud Self-Confidence and sin.'[6] Speaking from an economic perspective, Eve

---

6. Diane Elizabeth Dreher, 'Milton's Warning to Puritans in *Paradise Lost*: Another Look at the Separation Scene', *Christianity and Literature* 41, no. 1 (1991), pp. 35–36.

says that the day ends quickly with little being done. Adam, however, believes there should be a balance between labour and rest.[7] Eve's mistaken motivation is a warning to workaholics who place productivity above love and obedience.

Adam reluctantly lets Eve go but makes her promise to return by noon:

> *Oft he to her his charge of quick return*
> *Repeated, she to him as oft engaged*
> *To be returned by noon amid the bower,*
> *And all things in best order to invite*
> *Noontide repast, or afternoon's repose.*
>
> (*PL* IX.399-403)

Eve is supposed to return and make lunch. It turns out that this was 'the great tragically uneaten lunch in history'.[8] Both Eve and then Adam would proceed to eat the forbidden fruit. The Eve that left and the Eve that returned was a different person, no longer the gentle and innocent woman. With a great sense of doom, Milton laments:

> *O much deceived, much failing, hapless Eve,*
> *Of thy presumed return! event perverse!*
> *Thou never from that hour in Paradise*
> *Found'st either sweet repast, or sound repose;*
> *Such ambush hid among sweet flowers and shades*
> *Waited with hellish rancour imminent*
> *To intercept thy way, or send thee back*
> *Despoiled of innocence, of faith, of bliss.*
>
> (*PL* IX.404-11)

Since Eve has never encountered evil, she could not be suspicious of the serpent. She is merely credulous and naive, overwhelmed by the devil's eloquence. If she knew of the serpent's deceit, she would have resisted him. Perhaps Milton is presenting a 'moral paradox' regarding innocence and virtue.[9] The innocent is not capable of true virtue; it is

---

7. Maureen Quilligan, 'Freedom, Service, and the Trade in Slaves: The Problem of Labour in *Paradise Lost*', in Zunder, *Paradise Lost*, p. 184.
8. David Daiches, *Milton: Paradise Lost* (London: E. Arnold, 1983), p. 54.
9. Daiches, *Milton: Paradise Lost*, p. 55.

only in the struggle and resistance to evil that true virtue is cultivated. Thus the Fall was necessary to produce virtuous persons. Eve's fall was due to her credulity and Adam's fall was due to his love for her.[10] Unfortunately after the Fall, Adam is less sympathetic as the couple spend fruitless hours arguing and accusing each other.

Milton is determined to assert that the Fall was not God's fault even though he created the character and knows what is happening. Adam and Eve should have known better:

> *Of man, with strength entire, and free will armed,*
> *Complete to have discovered and repulsed*
> *Whatever wiles of foe or seeming friend.*
> *For still they knew, and ought to have still remembered*
> *The high injunction not to taste that fruit,*
> *Whoever tempted; which they not obeying,*
> *Incurred, what could they less, the penalty,*
> *And manifold in sin, deserved to fall.*
>
> (*PL* X.9-16)

After the Fall, Adam treats Eve harshly with bitter anger: 'Out of my sight, thou serpent, that name best / Befits thee with him leagued, thyself as false / And hateful' (*PL* X.867-69). However, Eve responds with gentleness and humility: 'Forsake me not thus, Adam, witness heaven / What love sincere, and reverence in my heart / I bear thee' (*PL* X.914-16). Adam responds with consolation and compassion, which is the beginning of their moral recovery, with a prayer to God to submit themselves to His will and mercy.

The punishment for their sin of disobedience is that they have to labour to earn their keep, and suffer pain in childbirth for a woman. However, work for Adam is a welcome relief from idleness: 'on me the curse aslope / Glanced on the ground, with labour I must earn / My bread; what harm? Idleness had been worse' (*PL* X.1053-55). Be that as it may, Adam asks why the rest of humankind, who are innocent, should suffer for his fault. The sin of Adam affects all generations: 'But all corrupt, both mind and will depraved' (*PL* X.825).

In Book XI, God sends the Archangel Michael to banish Adam and Eve from Paradise. Before their departure, Michael reveals a vision of

---

10. See also David V. Urban, 'The Falls of Satan, Eve, and Adam in John Milton's Paradise Lost: A Study in Insincerity', *Christianity and Literature* 67, no. 1 (2017), pp. 98–107.

the future to Adam, which is rather bleak and ominous. Nonetheless, we observe the growing humanity of our first parents, their fear and sorrow tempered by hope and resolution. In fact, Adam regards their Fall as fortunate: 'O goodness infinite, goodness immense / That all this good of evil shall produce, / And evil turn to good' (*PL* XII.469-71).

Milton attempts to rewrite and revise Scripture, especially in Book XII, which contains six speeches about biblical events by Archangel Michael, beginning with the aftermath of the Flood and ending with the Second Coming. From these lessons, Adam learns how his sin of disobedience has affected him and the rest of humankind. Scripture suggests the need humans have for God, whereas Milton maintains in *Paradise Lost* that humans must also depend on one another, thus transforming 'Biblical divine paternalism into poetical human interdependence, one culminating in political society.'[11] This transformation suggests religious and political emancipation. Obedience to God must be supplemented by human intelligence. While the Bible narrates the past, *Paradise Lost* is progressive as it looks toward the future, life beyond Eden.

Paradoxically, the Fall was a fortunate event because it enabled human beings to be equipped with the knowledge to fight against the forces of evil and thus prove their worth. It also provides seasonal work for farmers, intellectual work for scholars and creative work for artists. Michael reminds Adam that tyranny is inevitable in the fallen world, but a mature person cannot remain ignorant of evil. Paradise may be lost, but a challenging world awaits them for cultivation and development.[12]

## Augustinian Influence

Influenced and inspired by Augustine's *City of God*, the main theme of Milton's *Paradise Lost* is simple and universal – our happiness lies in obeying God's will. To do otherwise would only bring us miseries and sadness.[13] It is based on the understanding that, without exception, God created all things good, and evil is merely a privation of good. God says to Adam, 'I made him just and right, / Sufficient to have stood,

---

11. Paul M. Dowling, 'Paradise Lost and Politics Gained: Milton Rewrites Scripture', *Cithara* 44, no. 2 (2005), p. 16.
12. Daiches, *Milton: Paradise Lost*, p. 62.
13. This section is a summary of C. S. Lewis, *A Preface to Paradise Lost* (London: Oxford University Press, 1960), pp. 66–72. See Peter Amadeus Fiore, *Milton and Augustine: Patterns of Augustinian Thought in Paradise Lost* (University Park, PA: Pennsylvania State University, 2022).

though free to fall. / Such I created all the ethereal powers' (*PL* III.98-100). The angel says: 'O Adam, one almighty is, from whom / All things proceed, and up to him return, / If not depraved from good, created all / Such to perfection' (*PL* V.469-72).

Thus what we regard as evil is a perversion of the good, which takes place when a creature is more interested in itself than in God, wishing to exist on its own, committing the sin of pride. According to Augustine, Satan is 'that proud angel, whose very pride made him envious and also caused him to turn from God to follow himself. With the arrogance, as it were, of a tyrant, he chose to rejoice over subjects rather than to be a subject himself; and consequently fell from the spiritual paradise' (*City of God*, 14.11).[14] Milton describes Satan as 'thought himself impaired' (*PL* V.665). Satan is portrayed as a tyrant, concerned only with his own dignity, attempting to maintain his independence and claiming he is 'self-begot, self-raised' (*PL* V.860), thus denying that he is created by God.

Augustine asserts that good can exist without evil, but evil cannot exist without good (*City of God*, 14.11). Having the same nature, both good and bad angels are happy only when they are obedient to God and unhappy when they adhere to themselves:

> For while the good angels steadfastly remain in the good that is shared by all – in their case this is God himself – and so enjoy his eternity, truth and love, the bad angels, exulting rather in their own power, as though they themselves were their own good, sank from the higher good that brings happiness and is shared by all to the level of merely private good. (*City of God*, 12.1)

Thus in *Paradise Lost*, Satan has not lost his nature which is fundamentally good because he was created by God; otherwise he would not have existed. It is only his *will* that is perverted: 'his form had yet not lost All her original brightness, nor appeared / Less than archangel ruined, and the excess / Of glory obscured' (*PL* I. 591-94).

Even though God has made all creatures good, He knows that some will voluntarily disobey Him and thus make themselves bad. However, through their evil deeds, He will bring out the good. Just as He has

---

14. The quotations in this chapter are taken from Augustine, *City of God*, tr. William M. Green, Loeb Classical Library 417 (Cambridge, MA: Harvard University Press, 1972).

shown His love in creating good natures, He will show justice in using evil wills: 'Just as God is superlatively good as creator of good natures, so he is superlatively just as regulator of evil wills. The result is that when evil wills make ill use of good natures, he himself makes a good use even of evil wills' (*City of God*, 11.17). This doctrine of Augustine is reflected in *Paradise Lost* when we witness how Satan seeks to pervert humankind. God utilises this perversion, so Satan's intention falls flat: 'his evil / Thou usest, and from thence creat'st more good' (*PL* VII.615-16). Thus in the end, Adam is amazed and exclaims, 'That all this good of evil shall produce, / And evil turn to good' (*PL* XII.470-71). God subverts Satan's plan, drawing good out of evil, and an apparent misfortune turns out to be good, *Felix culpa* (happy fault). Given the freedom to do evil, Satan finds that he has unwittingly produced good, and 'those who will not be God's sons become His tools'.[15]

Milton agrees with Augustine, who teaches that, if the human race had not fallen, they would have been promoted to angels (*City of God*, 14.10): 'Of men innumerable, there to dwell, / Not here, till by degrees of merit raised / They open to themselves at length the way' (*PL* VII.156-58). There will come a time when our human 'bodies may at last turn all to spirit … winged ascend' (*PL* V.497-98).

Believing women to be the weaker sex, Satan attacks Eve, who is supposed to be less intelligent and more gullible (*City of God*, 14.11). Milton's Satan is pleased to find 'The woman, opportune to all attempts, / Her husband, for I view far round, not nigh, / Whose higher intellectual more I shun' (*PL* IX.481-83). However, Adam is not deceived but chooses to be with her due to a social bond (*City of God*, 14.11). Milton puts it this way: 'Against his better knowledge, not deceived, / But fondly overcome with female charm' (*PL* IX.998-99). Adam simply could not live without his wife.

The Fall is due to disobedience – the fruit is harmful because it was forbidden. God forbids it as a way to teach or test obedience: 'God's command and obedience was enjoined; and this virtue is, in a sense, the mother and guardian of all virtues in a rational creature, inasmuch as man has been naturally so created that it is advantageous for him to be submissive but ruinous to follow his own will and not the will of his creator' (*City of God*, 14.12). In her dream, Eve believes it is a 'fruit divine' fit for the gods (*PL* V.67). In truth, the fruit is the pledge and sign of human obedience to God (*PL* III.95, IV.428). Since obedience, the sole command of God, is easy to follow, it is a serious sin if we break it.

---

15. Lewis, *A Preface to Paradise Lost*, p. 68.

As mentioned, the Fall results from disobeying God's single command. Satan approaches Eve and gains her confidence through her pride and by flattering her beauty. Encouraging Eve to disobey God, Satan tells her that God forbids eating that fruit to keep His worshippers low and ignorant, thus encouraging her to be on her own, to be selfish (*PL* IX.703-04).

According to Augustine, to sin is to turn away from God and towards oneself. It is selfishness which is pride itself. He writes: 'What is pride but a craving for perverse elevation? For it is perverse elevation to forsake the ground in which the mind ought to be rooted, and to become and be, in a sense, grounded in oneself' (*City of God*, 14.13). Since the self is made from nothing, selfishness results in unhappiness:

> Yet the being that can be happy cannot draw happiness from himself, since he was created out of nothing, but from him by whom he was created. For the attainment of this good makes such a being happy, just as the loss of it makes him unhappy. But he whose happiness comes from his own good self rather than from an alien good cannot be unhappy because he cannot lose this self. (*City of God*, 12.1)

Disobedience results in humanity's loss of authority over inferior things, namely the passions and emotions, and with it they 'became carnal in mind as well' (*City of God*, 12.1, p. 347). Thus, his powers are 'lapsed', 'though forfeit and enthralled / By sin to foul exorbitant desires' (*PL* III.176-77). After the Fall, rationality ceased to rule, and the will did not listen to reason: 'For understanding ruled not, and the will / Heard not her lore, both in subjection now / To sensual appetite, who from beneath / Usurping over sovereign reason claimed' (*PL* IX.1127-30); 'Reason in man obscured, or not obeyed, / Immediately inordinate desires / And upstart passions catch the government' (*PL* XII.86-88). This applies especially to the area of sexuality: love turns to lust after the Fall.

## Role of Reason

For Milton, freedom has to serve reason; otherwise, it is not freedom at all. He calls it 'true filial freedom', which implies obedience. Regarding the nature of Adam and Eve, he writes:

> *For in their looks divine*
> *The image of their glorious maker shone,*
> *Truth, wisdom, sanctitude severe and pure,*

> *Severe but in true filial freedom placed;*
> *Whence true authority in men.*
>
> (*PL* IV. 291-95)

We are born free to follow our reason, leading us to obey God. If we go against reason, we abuse our freedom. Reason leads to God, who also gives us free will to reject Him. To be reasonable is to be obedient to God, but we can also choose to be unreasonable.[16] Choice is thus connected to right reason and loving obedience. Michael explains the relationship between liberty and reason to the fallen Adam:

> *Since thy original lapse, true liberty*
> *Is lost, which always with right reason dwells*
> *Twinned, and from her hath no dividual being:*
>
> (*PL* XII. 83-85)

In the heavenly council, God's desire is to see his angels and humans responding to him in loving obedience: 'Not free, what proof could they have given sincere / Of true allegiance, constant faith or love, / Where only what they needs must do, appeared' (*PL* III.103-05); 'Reason also is choice' (*PL* III.108).

Just before the temptation scene, Adam warns Eve regarding what God has forbidden: 'But God left free the will, for what obeys / Reason, is free, and reason he made right' (*PL* IX.351-52). In his emphasis on the freedom of human beings to choose, Milton highlights the importance of making rational choices with loving obedience to God as the only path to find true happiness and rest.[17]

In his plot to deceive Eve with spurious reasoning, Satan asks:

> *Knowledge forbidden? Suspicious, reasonless.*
> *Why should their Lord*
> *Envy them that? can it be sin to know,*
> *Can it be death? and do they only stand*
> *By ignorance, is that their happy state,*
> *The proof of their obedience and their faith?*
>
> (*PL* IV.515-20)

---

16. John S. Reist, 'Reason as a Theological-Apologetic Motif in Milton's Paradise Lost', *Canadian Journal of Theology* 16, no. 3-4 (1970), p. 241.
17. Daniel Ritchie and Jared Hedges, 'Choosing Rest in *Paradise Lost*', *Christianity and Literature* 67, no. 2 (2018), p. 272.

With cunning deceit, Satan tells Eve that she would be like God if she ate the fruit. The issue here is not merely about eating a fruit and gaining knowledge, but being disobedient to God's command. Sin, thus, is 'pure disobedience'.[18] In fact, gaining knowledge is a Christian duty, as Milton dedicated his whole life in the pursuit of truth to the extent of losing his eyesight. However, he believes ultimately that human knowledge is for glorifying God, and that it is subject to His authority.

True reasoning for Milton is a 'moral virtue' coming from proper education which 'fits a man to perform justly, skilfully, and magnanimously all the offices, both private and public, of peace and war'.[19] He believes that virtue grounded in right reasoning is where happiness can be found. Thus, the Fall is the result of disobedience, not the attainment of knowledge:

> *I now must change*
> *Those notes to tragic; foul distrust, and breach*
> *Disloyal on the part of man, revolt,*
> *And disobedience*
>
> (*PL* IX.5-8)

In Book XII, Milton elaborates on the severity of disobedience as an offence against God. Michael praises Abraham because he obeys and believes in God without knowing what land he would be going to (*PL* XII.126-27). Adam and Eve would have remained free if they had obeyed; but deceived by Satan, Eve believed she could gain knowledge and become a god. God blames Adam for his uxoriousness: 'Was she thy God, that her thou didst obey / Before his voice' (*PL* X.145-46). Adam has a free choice, to fall or not to fall:

> *They trespass, authors to themselves in all*
> *Both what they judge and what they choose; for so*
> *I formed them free, and free they must remain,*
> *Till they enthrall themselves: I else must change*
> *Their nature, and revoke the high decree*
> *Unchangeable, eternal, which ordained*
> *Their freedom*
>
> (*PL* III.122-28)

---

18. Reist, 'Reason', p. 242.
19. Quoted in Reist, 'Reason', p. 243.

The Renaissance concept of man is an individual who is a free human being, capable of reasoning in order to live a life of dignity and happiness.[20] Since Adam and Eve failed to obey, the consequences were severe:

> *Yet know withal,*
> *Since thy original lapse, true liberty*
> *Is lost, which always with right reason dwells*
> *Twinned, and from her hath no dividual being:*
> *Reason in man obscured, or not obeyed,*
> *Immediately inordinate desires*
> *And upstart passions catch the government*
> *From reason, and to servitude reduce*
> *Man till then free.*
>
> (*PL* XII.82-90)

Even though they have disobeyed and are punished, God did not strip them of the power of reasoning. Hence, the children of Adam and Eve still maintain their ability to understand and distinguish between good and evil. In other words, they are stripped of innocence and happiness, but not reason and rationality.

## Spellbound by Satan

In the book of Genesis, Satan is not mentioned as the tempter, only a talking snake. In fact, Satan appears in the Bible only a few times: in the book of Job as a devious character in the Heavenly Court and in the Gospels as the tempter of Jesus Christ in the wilderness (Luke 4:1-14; Matt. 4:1-11; Mark 1:11-13). According to the book of Revelation, 'And the great dragon was cast out, that old serpent called the Devil, and Satan, which deceiveth the whole world: he was cast out into the earth, and his angels were cast out with him' (12:9).[21]

Besides the Scripture, Milton's portrayal of Satan is drawn from other apocryphal and patristic sources, which makes him the most fascinating and memorable character in *Paradise Lost*. Conscious of our own sinfulness and brokenness, we can easily identify with Satan's tortured psyche, deep sense of anger, bitterness, hatred and his Satanic

---

20. Reist, 'Reason', p. 244.
21. Scripture quotations in this chapter are taken from the King James Version.

viewpoint.[22] Spellbound by his grand speeches, we see Satan as a tragic hero who evokes sympathy.

Dominating the first two books, Satan gives us one of the most famous lines in English literature: 'Better to reign in hell, than serve in heaven' (*PL* I.263). Capable of jealousy, despair and remorse, he sheds 'tears such as angels weep' (*PL* I.620) even though he is hell-bent on seducing Eve as a serpent. In fact, we first meet him as 'the infernal serpent' (*PL* I.34) and later as the 'first grand thief' (*PL* IV.192), like the wolves in John 10:12. Satan is even regarded as a theologian, albeit a heretical one.

## Satanic Verses

In the New Testament, the devil Satan is known as a liar or the father of lies. Nonetheless, in *Paradise Lost*, we need to take his portrayal of God seriously to understand him as a heretic. In fact, Karl Barth says that the serpent is the first theologian in the world despite his bad theology or heresy. Justin Martyr and Irenaeus insist that heresies are the result of Satanic influence, while Tertullian believes that heretical interpretation of Scripture is the work of the devil. Augustine also asserts that the devil inspires heresies within the Church. Heretics are known as apostate, and the chief apostate is Satan himself.[23] In *Paradise Lost*, as the first theologian, Satan speaks blasphemously against God: 'Artificer of fraud; and was the first / That practised falsehood under saintly show' (*PL* IV.121-22). However, as a political orator, Satan also speaks of God's decree, freedom of angels and liberty (*PL* V.772-802).

After being expelled from Heaven, the fallen angels begin to theologise, portraying God as a tyrant whose absolute power is used to suppress his creatures. This depiction of God is a projection of Satan's character.[24] Ludwig Feuerbach asserts that the Christian God is a projection of human thinking: 'Consciousness of God is self-consciousness, knowledge of God is self-knowledge.'[25] In the same way, Satanic theology is the devil's perception of God.

---

22. Charles Martindale, *John Milton and the Transformation of Ancient Epic* (London: Croom Helm, 1986), p. 39. See also Stanley Eugene Fish, *Surprised by Sin: The Reader in* Paradise Lost (London: Macmillan, 1967).
23. Benjamin Myers, *Milton's Theology of Freedom* (Berlin: Walter de Gruyter, 2006), pp. 54–55.
24. Myers, *Milton's Theology of Freedom*, p. 57.
25. Ludwig Feuerbach and George Eliot, *The Essence of Christianity*, 2nd ed. (New York: Calvin Blanchard, 1855), p. 33.

Satan acknowledges God as the 'potent victor' (*PL* I.95), 'the conqueror' (*PL* I.323) and 'monarch' (*PL* I.638). Regarding God as the powerful victor, Satan says he will inflict misery and ruin on his enemies, consigning them to a 'dungeon' (*PL* II.317) 'in strictest bondage' (*PL* II.321). Filled with 'vengeful ire' (*PL* I.148), Satan holds that God is willing to let his enemies live so that they suffer longer, thus meeting his desire for revenge:

> *But what if he our conqueror (whom I now*
> *Of force believe almighty, since no less*
> *Than such could have o'erpowered such force as ours)*
> *Have left us this our spirit and strength entire*
> *Strongly to suffer and support our pains,*
> *That we may so suffice his vengeful ire.*
>
> (*PL* I.143-48)

Indeed, God is portrayed by Satan as a sadistic deity who finds satisfaction in oppressing and torturing those who turn against him.

Compared to the horrors of Dante's Inferno, Milton's Hell is characterised by 'silence and absence', devoid of physical tortures.[26] In his Hell, the devils are given freedom to build a palace, organise council meetings and play music. Satan even admits that Hell is not so much a place as the state of his own 'mind':

> *A mind not to be changed by place or time.*
> *The mind is its own place, and in itself*
> *Can make a heaven of hell, a hell of heaven.*
>
> (*PL* I.253-55)

Regarding the fall of the angels, Satan blames God, who he says is directly responsible: 'Put forth at full, but still his strength concealed, / Which tempted our attempt, and wrought our fall' (*PL* I.641-42). In other words, it is God who causes them to sin and then punishes them for this transgression. As Nietzsche says about the tyrant who 'will[s] to power', Satan's description of God appears to be like an omnipotent despot with absolute control over his creatures. Nevertheless, as we know, it is Satan who decides to challenge God and receives the punishment he deserves. Just as he himself is hell, he becomes the serpent in which he disguises himself.

---

26. Myers, *Milton's Theology of Freedom*, p. 59.

## 'Punished in the Shape he Sinned'

Angel Gabriel reminds Satan that he was once a servant in Heaven, 'Once fawned, and cringed, and servilely adored / Heaven's awful monarch; (*PL* IV.959-60). However, we remember him most vividly as a rebellious angel who regards God, his creator, as a tyrant. He fights a heroic battle, undertakes a dangerous journey through Chaos to Eden to corrupt humankind, and returns to Hell in triumph, feeling very pleased with himself. The irony is that his victory speech becomes a hiss – no longer a beautiful angel, he becomes what was his disguise – a serpent. His fellow demons return 'hiss for hiss. . . with forkèd tongue / To forkèd tongue' (*PL* X.518-19). His anticipated bliss turns out to be a hiss.[27]

Satan was 'punished in the shape he sinned' (*PL* X.516) and so were the rest of the demons. This punishment alludes to the plight of the thieves in Dante's *Inferno* 24 and 25, where we witness serpents stealing their bodies, which reflects the sin they have committed on earth. As mentioned in the previous chapter, this literary device is known as *contrapasso* – the punishment fitting the sin. 'God justice is poetic justice' in that his punishment of the sinners is appropriate for their offences.[28] This is confirmed by Satan when he says 'myself am hell' (*PL* IV.75). The devils who rebel against God are punished when they choose a tyrant to lead them.

Influenced by *The Divine Comedy*, 'Milton's devils enact in sequence the variety of evils that Dante's condemned souls perpetually re-enact fixed in their several rungs.'[29] Like Dante's *Inferno*, the use of *contrapasso* by Milton reveals the sins of the devils as well as unrepentant sinners. Of course, Satan's first offence is the sin of physical deception.[30] Through Satan, Milton shows the gradual weakening of the sinner's will until it is completely destroyed. Satan deceives himself when he believes his 'unconquerable will' is capable of defeating God.

---

27. Neil Forsyth, 'Satan', in Louis Schwartz (ed.), *The Cambridge Companion to Paradise Lost* (Cambridge: Cambridge University Press, 2014), p. 18.
28. Ethan Smilie, 'Satan's Unconquerable Will and Milton's Use of Dantean Contrapasso in Paradise Lost,' *Renascence* 65, no. 2 (2013), p. 91.
29. Irene Samuel, *Dante and Milton: The Commedia and Paradise Lost* (Ithaca, NY: Cornell University Press, 1966), p. 73.
30. Smilie, 'Satan's Unconquerable Will', p. 101.

Nine days after their fall from Heaven, Satan and his fellow demons 'Lay vanquished, rolling in the fiery gulf' (*PL* I.52). Here is an insight into his mind:

> *For now the thought*
> *Both of lost happiness and lasting pain*
> *Torments him; round he throws his baleful eyes*
> *That witnessed huge affliction and dismay*
> *Mixed with obdurate pride and steadfast hate*
>
> (*PL* I.54-58)

Hell is seen through Satan's lens as he perceives it to be a product of his thought. Like Paradise, Hell is both a place and a state of mind – Satan is Hell itself. As a place, it is 'A dungeon horrible, on all sides round / As one great furnace flamed, yet from those flames / No light, but rather darkness visible / Served only to discover sights of woe' (*PL* I.61-64).

Relying on the classics and Judaeo-Christian tradition, Milton deftly develops his vision of Hell seen through Satan's eyes.[31] Images of darkness and light fill the poem with paradoxes or contradictions, such as 'darkness visible', alluding to Scripture 'where light is like darkness' in the description of the inferno. The development of the devil comes from Isaiah, 'How art thou fallen from heaven, O Lucifer, son of the morning! how art thou cut down to the ground, which didst weaken the nations!' ( Isa. 14:12). These words in Isaiah, spoken to the King of Babylon, are borrowed from an ancient legend about a deity who attempts to rule over the stars in heavenly court, but is thrown into Sheol – like Satan who seeks to be like God is hurled into the pit. In the Gospel, Jesus tells his disciples, 'I beheld Satan as lightning fall from heaven' (Luke 10:18). The biblical allusions place Milton's *Paradise Lost* firmly in the Christian patristic tradition. Echoes of Virgil, allusions to *The Aeneid*, provide *Paradise Lost* with a classical foundation with added resonance.[32]

After the disastrous fall, Satan regains his consciousness and reinvents himself with a grand speech filled with defiance and passion, boasting of his 'unconquerable will, / And study of revenge, immortal hate, / And courage never to submit or yield' (*PL* I.106-08). In spite of his defeat and despair, he hopes for a more successful battle. Incapable of repentance

---

31. Forsyth , 'Satan', p. 19.
32. Charles Martindale, *John Milton and the Transformation of Ancient Epic* (London: Croom Helm, 1986), p. 4.

and beyond redemption, with his mind fixed, Satan appears pitiful. Sadly for him, 'rest can never dwell, hope never comes / That comes to all' (*PL* I.66-67), reminding us of the inscription at the Gate of Dante's Inferno, 'Abandon all hope, ye who enter here.' It is no surprise Satan's speech is marked by contradiction and confusion.

Satan plans to subvert God's creation 'out of good still to find means of evil ' (*PL* I.165). The depth of Satanic being is Hell itself. He confirms, 'Which way I fly is hell; myself am hell; / And in the lowest deep a lower deep / Still threatening to devour me opens wide' (*PL* IV.75-77). His soliloquy of self-exploration and self-accusation makes him a tragic hero. The first ten lines (*PL* IV.32-41) allude to Greek tragedies, Aeschylus's *Prometheus Bound* and *Phoenissae* by Euripides. On the other hand, regarding speech and rhetorical techniques to portray the character's inwardness, English drama (Gardner) was more important in influencing Milton.[33] Satan's tortured soliloquy strikes a chord with Hamlet's tormented brooding. In this self-examination, Satan realises that it was wrong to rebel against God, but there is no return for him (*PL* IV.42-43).

From the 'immortal hatred' (*PL* I.107) of God, Satan turns to hatred of humankind. In fact, he becomes the personification of hatred. He hates the sunbeam because it reminds him of his shining status in Heaven, and he curses himself (*PL* IV.71). Envious of the love between Adam and Eve, he acknowledges that he could have loved them, but chooses to destroy them. Torn between love and hate, Satan chooses to hate in his free choice. Be that as it may, Satan hesitates when he sees the beauty and innocence of Eve (*PL* IX.489-91). Soon, fierce hatred consumes him as he recollects and regains his strength to pervert his prey. He needs to talk himself back to hatred when he finds himself vacillating in doing evil. Master of rhetoric, Satan convinces Eve to eat the forbidden fruit even though she finds it strange that a snake could speak.

In Hebrew, Satan is known as the adversary; in Greek, he is known as the devil, *diabolos*, which means opponent. In *Paradise Lost*, Satan is the 'arch-enemy' (*PL* I.81). The origin of evil is a favourite topic among theologians and early Church Fathers, such as Augustine. The story of the Fall – rebellion in Heaven – has its roots in ancient myths and Jewish sacred literature. The Old Testament includes the story of Leviathan (Job 41:1) and the passage in Ezekiel 28 regarding the Prince of Tyre. Following Origen and Augustine, the story of the cosmic battle in *Paradise Lost* reveals Milton's effort in baptising or Christianising ancient legends and myths. A resonance with Manichaeanism is found in Milton's depiction

---

33. Forsyth , 'Satan', p. 23.

of the eternal conflict between light and darkness.[34] Since he is creating a literary work, which falls outside ecclesiastical sanction, Milton has the poetic freedom to embellish his story with esoteric details.

## Literary Myth

*Paradise Lost* can be read as a literary myth from a phenomenological perspective. Such an approach clarifies Milton's treatment of moral absolutes, reveals the importance of grace over faith and works, and justifies temporal confusion in the poem. Myth is a 'verbal presentation' 'replete with power'. Concerned with primeval time, 'events are juxtaposed as types rather than arranged in a cause and effect or chronological sequence'.[35] For example, in *Paradise Lost*, the fall of humankind occurs before the incarnation, but later we witness Christ willing to sacrifice himself, which leads God to promote him. This results in Satan's jealousy and rebellion. Such chronological confusion is acceptable if we read the epic poem as literary myth and types, a juxtaposition of events.

Further, understanding *Paradise Lost* as a phenomenological myth allows us to identify God as 'wholly other' and above moral categories:

> *Thee Father first they sung omnipotent,*
> *Immutable, immortal, infinite,*
> *Eternal king; thee author of all being,*
> *Fountain of light, thyself invisible*
>
> (*PL* III.372-75)

When God is regarded as omnipotent, Satan is no match for Him, no longer an adversary. The struggle between Satan and God is for the purpose of bringing forth the good out of evil. Satan's rebellion causes God to create human beings in His own image. The disobedience of humans leads to the incarnation of Christ. A phenomenological reading of *Paradise Lost* enables us to see God as an almighty power, and the importance of grace for our salvation. We understand this poem's historical events as a literary myth that relates to the past and the future.[36]

---

34. Forsyth, 'Satan', pp. 25, 27.
35. J. R. Brink, '*Paradise Lost* as Literary Myth', *Cithara* 22, no. 1 (1982), p. 14.
36. Brink, '*Paradise Lost* as Literary Myth', p. 21.

The Fall as a literary myth consists of three main teachings: preternatural world, original sin and redemption. These three doctrines are related to the themes of 'separation, initiation and return' which are common features in mythical discourse. Augustine interprets this mythic pattern within the framework of salvation history: the short-lived ideal life in the Garden, the exile following the Fall and Paradise regained.[37] We can locate Milton's *Paradise Lost* within this threefold model.

The events in *Paradise Lost* have also been interpreted as reflecting the political situation in seventeenth-century England. Satan has been compared to Charles I and Cromwell.[38] It is a modern warfare that Satan fights as he invents gunpowder. Neil Forsyth writes, 'Thus warfare itself passes from the heroic code of classical epic to the logistical battles of the modern world, where what wins is not courage but superior firepower, and where the enemy is always depersonalized, even demonized.'[39]

Placing their trust in armament and weaponry, the devils believe physical force is the decisive factor in their battle against God.[40] In fact, Warren Chernaik maintains that 'In *Paradise Lost*, most of the references to "strength", especially in Books I, II, and VI, are to physical strength alone, showing a refusal by Satan and his followers to admit any moral dimension.'[41] In response to Abdiel's appeal to humility and obedience, Satan asserts his own 'puissance' (*PL* V.864). Satan sees God as a powerful deity in the physical sense, and thus he responds using violence. Michael, however, recognises that war has no place in Paradise: 'Heaven the seat of bliss / Brooks not the works of violence and war' (*PL* VI.273-74). Violence will only lead to pain and sufferings: 'Mangled with ghastly wounds through plate and mail' (*PL* VI.368).

---

37. Peter Amadeus Fiore, *Milton and Augustine: Patterns of Augustinian Thought in Paradise Lost* (University Park, PA: Pennsylvania State University, 2022), p. 1.
38. Warren Chernaik, 'Monarchy and Servitude: The Politics of *Paradise Lost*', in Chernaik, *Milton and the Burden of Freedom* (Cambridge: Cambridge University Press, 2017), p. 128.
39. Forsyth , 'Satan', p. 26. See also Christopher Hill, '*Paradise Lost* and the English Revolution', in Zunder, *Paradise Lost*, pp. 15–27.
40. Stephen M. Fallon, '*Paradise Lost* and the Materialism Debate', *Continuum* (St Xavier College, Chicago) 3 (1994), p. 194.
41. Warren Chernaik, 'God's Just Yoke: Power and Justice in *Paradise Lost*', in Chernaik, *Milton and the Burden of Freedom*, p. 148.

Milton places the war at the centre of his poem, which is the experience of his age, as well as ours. In fact, the cosmic struggle and the origin of sin could be understood in contemporary political terms. *Paradise Lost* is progressive as it looks toward the future, life beyond Eden. We have indeed lost our paradise. The need for a messiah in our modern world is more urgent than ever before.

# Chapter 5

# *The Rime of the Ancient Mariner*

## Samuel Taylor Coleridge (1772-1834)

Samuel Taylor Coleridge, lyrical poet, critic and philosopher, was born the son of an Anglican parson in Ottery St Mary, Devon, England. He studied at Christ's Hospital in 1782 and then at Jesus College, Cambridge, in 1791. At school and college, Coleridge read widely and deeply on literature and philosophy that deals with the imagination. Plagued by mounting debts, and involved in radical politics and Unitarian beliefs, he did not find life at Cambridge smooth sailing. Despite being unfit for military life, he enlisted in the 15th Light Dragoon at Reading under the pseudonym Silas Tomkyn Comberbache (STC) in December 1793, hoping to evade the burden of debt. With difficulty, his brothers secured his release from the army, and he was permitted to continue his studies at Cambridge. Nevertheless, in 1794, he left the university without graduating.

Coleridge and William Wordsworth had a deep and lasting friendship. In 1798, the publication of their *Lyrical Ballads* marked the beginning of the English Romantic movement. This collection included *The Rime of the Ancient Mariner*. The poem, written during the autumn and winter of 1797-98, is considered to be Coleridge's masterpiece. It reveals him to be a writer with visionary imagination, lyrical beauty and profound philosophical insight. Like all great works of literature, *The Ancient Mariner* is open to many levels of interpretation. Framed within a Christian mythic structure with religious symbolism, this poem is also an expression of the human condition, seeking for salvation while faced with evil forces. In *Biographia Literaria*, published in 1817, Coleridge believes that the first principle of philosophy is best expressed in spiritual terms rather than by a 'materialist's creed'. His main interest, as far as the imagination is concerned, lies with the Logos or Word, identified as Christ in the Scriptures.[1]

This chapter explores the journey of the Mariner, from crime, contrition, confession and finally, to conversion. It attempts to interpret this poem as reflecting the fall and redemption of humanity. Just as the sin of our first parents is more than eating a fruit, the sin of the Mariner is more than just killing a bird.

## The Mariner and His Story

The poem's protagonist is the Ancient Mariner. He enthrals and appals a young man with a story about his sea voyage. The young man is one of three guests en route to a wedding feast. The Mariner mesmerises and prevents this wedding-guest from enjoying the festivities until, at the end of the poem, he loses complete interest. The following day, the young man wakes up a sadder but wiser person. Perhaps the Mariner's interruption suggests that such celebration is not as important as what he is going to tell – a tale of fall and redemption. He describes how his ship leaves the harbour and sails south across the equator. A storm drives the vessel for days and nights until it gets stuck in the Antarctic region. The Mariner and his crew then see a friendly albatross. Without any reason, the Mariner acts on impulse and shoots the albatross with a crossbow:

> *And I had done a hellish thing,*
> *And it would work 'em woe:*
> *For all averred, I had killed the bird*
> *That made the breeze to blow.*
> *Ah wretch! said they, the bird to slay,*
> *That made the breeze to blow!* (91-96)[2]

---

1. James Engell, 'Biographia Literaria', in Lucy Newlyn (ed.), *The Cambridge Companion to Coleridge* (Cambridge: Cambridge University Press, 2002), p. 64.
2. Quotations in this chapter are from the 1817 text in Samuel Taylor Coleridge and Paul H. Fry, *The Rime of the Ancient Mariner: Complete, Authoritative Texts of the 1798 and 1817 Versions with Biographical and*

The shooting of the albatross is the turning point in the poem – 'it gathers weight and consequence and becomes a sign and emblem of the whole mystery of evil and the strange self-destructing nature of fallen humanity'.[3] The Mariner's admission, 'I had done a hellish thing', reveals the seriousness of the offence, a trespass that goes beyond the accusation of his shipmates. On hearing what he has done, the shipmates congratulate the Mariner for killing the bird: 'Twas right, said they, such birds to slay, / That bring the fog and mist' (101-02). Although they subsequently condemn the Mariner with 'evil looks' (139), by their initial congratulation they make themselves accomplices in the crime. This trespass is a violation of nature, and springs from valuing the albatross purely as an instrument in guiding the ship rather than as part of God's creation.

## Humankind and Nature

The violation of nature can be traced to the Old Testament in relation to human's domination of creation: 'Then God said, "Let us make humankind in our image, according to our likeness; and let them have dominion over the fish of the sea, and over the birds of the air, and over the cattle, and over all the wild animals of the earth, and over every creeping thing that creeps upon the earth"' (Gen. 1:26). 'God blessed them, and God said to them, "Be fruitful and multiply, and fill the earth and subdue it; and have dominion over the fish of the sea and over the birds of the air and over every living thing that moves upon the earth"' (Gen. 1:28). Further, God gives Adam the power to name all the creatures of the earth and thus places him on top of creation. Such a privilege eventually led to manipulation of the natural world.[4]

Coleridge believes that, if we are open to nature's influence, we will recognise God in it and find true happiness and understanding of the beauty of our universe. God speaks to us through nature, but we have the free will to listen or not to listen. In other words, we can shut ourselves away from nature's influence consciously or unconsciously. Coleridge, in his 'Religious Musings', has maintained that 'if man is

---

*Historical Contexts, Critical History, and Essays from Contemporary Critical Perspectives* (Boston: Bedford/St Martin's, 1999).

3. Malcolm Guite, *Mariner: A Voyage with Samuel Taylor Coleridge* (London: Hodder & Stoughton, 2017), p. 175.
4. Donald J. Moores, '"Oh Happy Living Things": Healing Serpent Power in Coleridge's "Rime"', *Studies in Spirituality* 17 (2007), p. 228.

blind to the presence of divine light in nature, he is left with his own self-imposed darkness which he in turn projects on nature so that he becomes "A sordid solitary thing ... / Feeling himself, his own low self the whole", surrounded by a nature that is no more than an extension of his own mind, his own dejection or fear'.[5] This is what happens to the Mariner – alienated from nature and God as he suffers the consequences of his senseless shooting of a bird.

The treatment of nature in *The Ancient Mariner* corresponds to the Egyptians' attitude towards creation in the Wisdom of Solomon: 'For all people who were ignorant of God were foolish by nature; and they were unable from the good things that are seen to know the one who exists, nor did they recognize the artisan while paying heed to his works' (13:1). Alienation from nature is tantamount to alienation from God himself. The arrogant Egyptians attempt to rebuild the world in their own image:

> *For not even the inner chamber that held them protected them*
>     *from fear,*
> *but terrifying sounds rang out around them,*
> *and dismal phantoms with gloomy faces appeared.*
> *And no power of fire was able to give light,*
> *nor did the brilliant flames of the stars*
> *avail to illumine that hateful night.*
> *Nothing was shining through to them*
> *except a dreadful, self-kindled fire,*
> *and in terror they deemed the things that they saw*
>                                    (Wisdom 17:4-6)

Instead of appreciating the beauty of nature, these men experience nothing but their own fear caused by their sinfulness:

> *For even if nothing disturbing frightened them,*
> *yet, scared by the passing of wild animals and the hissing of*
>     *snakes*
> *they perished in trembling fear,*
> *refusing to look even at the air, though it nowhere could be*
>     *avoided.*

---

5. Quoted in Hendrik Roelof Rookmaaker, *Towards a Romantic Conception of Nature: Coleridge's Poetry up to 1803: A Study in the History of Ideas* (Amsterdam: John Benjamins Publishing Co., 1984), p. 69.

> *For wickedness is a cowardly thing, condemned by its own*
>   *testimony;*
> *distressed by conscience, it has always exaggerated the*
>   *difficulties*
>
> (Wisdom 17:9-11)

The similarities of ideas and images in *The Wisdom of Solomon* and *The Ancient Mariner* are striking and pertinent. The Mariner's world is frightening not because nature is nasty or vindictive; his fear is a projection of his guilt and remorse, which he fails to recognise. The poem can be interpreted as 'the dream all those who fail to perceive God's presence in nature are doomed to experience as reality'.[6] The Mariner represents the fate of those alienated from nature, experiencing the absence of God. The sea voyage is like a nightmare for the Mariner.

The passing of the spectre-ship results in the death of all 200 crew members. This ghost ship has two people on board, 'Death' and a woman who is 'The Nightmare Life-in-Death' (188, 194). Regarding the woman, the narrator says:

> *Her lips were red, her looks were free,*
> *Her locks were yellow as gold:*
> *Her skin was as white as leprosy,*
> *The Night-mair LIFE-IN-DEATH was she,*
> *Who thicks man's blood with cold.* (190-194)

The spectre woman, with skin as white as leprosy, plays dice for the sailors' lives. The image of leprosy also suggests that the apparent attractiveness of the lady becomes repulsive, a horrific nightmare.

## Images of Infection

Coleridge spoke against the evil of the slave trade in his public lectures. According to Tim Fulford, Coleridge writes about the Mariner on a slave-ship sailing towards the West Indies and entering a territory tainted with the 'diseases of the empire'.[7] This corruption spreads to the seas where 'the very deep did rot' (123).

---

6. Rookmaaker, *Romantic Conception of Nature*, p. 71.
7. Tim Fulford, 'Slavery and Superstition in the Supernatural Poems', in Newlyn, *Cambridge Companion to Coleridge*, p. 50.

Thus, *The Ancient Mariner* can be read as a mental as well as a physical voyage of exploration – 'the inward self could be staged outwardly, a form all could follow'. The inward self is also shaped by social and political conditions expressed in the poem, a reflection of Coleridge's political stance.[8] Critical of colonialism, Coleridge wrote 'Fears in Solitude':

> *From east to west*
> *A groan of accusation pierces Heaven!*
> *The wretched plead against us; multitudes*
> *Countless and vehement, the sons of God,*
> *Our brethren! Like a cloud that travels on,*
> *Steamed up from Cairo's swamps of pestilence,*
> *Even so, my countrymen! have we gone forth*
> *And borne to distant tribes slavery and pangs,*
> *And, deadlier far, our vices, whose deep taint*
> *With slow perdition murders the whole man,*
> *His body and his soul!* (43-53)

Attacking imperialism, Coleridge concludes that the British are more savage than the native people they colonised as they spread their own moral maladies – 'death-dealing corruption'.[9] In their exploration, the imperialists spread their deadly pestilence. Coleridge thus connects physical disease with the moral decadence of the British colonial enterprise. In sustaining slavery in the colonies, Britain exposed thousands of African natives and their own mariners to yellow fever, small pox, plague and other diseases. The leprosy of the spectre lady spreads to the sea as well. In fact, the Mariner, in his story, seems to suggest that the whole world is infected by his own experience of guilt and sin.

In the game of dice, the crew is the death prize, but the Mariner has been won by Night-Mair and continues to survive, living a life-in-death:

> *The naked hulk alongside came,*
> *And the twain were casting dice;*
> *'The game is done! I've won! I've won!'*
> *Quoth she, and whistles thrice.* (195-98)

While the Mariner looks at the Wedding-Guest with his own glittering eyes at the beginning of the poem, now each member of the crew curses him with his eyes:

---

8. Fulford, 'Slavery and Superstition', p. 49.
9. Fulford, 'Slavery and Superstition', p. 49.

> *One after one, by the star-dogged Moon,*
> *Too quick for groan or sigh,*
> *Each turned his face with a ghastly pang,*
> *And cursed me with his eye.* (216-19)

This is the punishment for killing the albatross, which the Mariner had the free will to refrain from doing. Further, as accomplices to the crime, and now subjected to the forces they have unleashed, the entire crew is condemned to die:

> *Four times fifty living men,*
> *(And I heard nor sigh nor groan)*
> *With heavy thump, a lifeless lump,*
> *They dropped down one by one.* (220-24)

Terrified by the tale of the Mariner, the Wedding-Guest responds:

> *[']I fear thee, ancient Mariner!*
> *I fear thy skinny hand!*
> *And thou art long, and lank, and brown,*
> *As is the ribbed sea-sand.*
>
> *I fear thee and thy glittering eye,*
> *And thy skinny hand, so brown.'–*
> *Fear not, fear not, thou Wedding-Guest!*
> *This body dropt not down.* (228-35)

The Wedding-Guest fears that the Mariner is one of the dead. The irony here is that the Mariner wishes to be dead rather than to be alone with the dead as he says:

> *Alone, alone, all, all alone,*
> *Alone on a wide wide sea!*
> *And never a saint took pity on*
> *My soul in agony* (236-39)

The sense of loneliness and isolation is even more prevalent and endemic in our time. Affecting both young and old, it is a profound kind of loneliness, a sense of alienation and agony that disconnects us from other people and the cosmos itself. The root cause of this sense of isolation is philosophical, reflecting our modern culture, which takes an instrumental or mechanistic view of nature. The occasional flashes of beauty we glimpse are only a mirage without meaning.[10] The Mariner's desperation, his experience of loneliness and pain, is also due to his inability to pray: 'A wicked whisper came, and made / My heart as dry as dust' (250-51).

## Guilt and Redemption

Related to this deep sense of loneliness is survival guilt which overwhelms the Mariner, since all the crew members are dead except the Mariner. For a week, the Mariner is alone, reflecting on his dreadful deed and the death of his crew. Eventually, the Mariner begins to understand and accept responsibility for his hideous act and says:

> *But oh! more horrible than that*
> *Is the curse in a dead man's eye!*
> *Seven days, seven nights, I saw that curse,*
> *And yet I could not die.* (263-66)

When the Mariner accepts his transgression, he begins to perceive the perfection of the universe. Marvelling at the beauty of nature, the Mariner blesses the water snakes. These snakes are no longer slimy parasites to be condemned but lovely creatures to be blessed:

> *O happy living things! no tongue*
> *Their beauty might declare:*
> *A spring of love gushed from my heart,*
> *And I blessed them unaware:*
> *Sure my kind saint took pity on me,*
> *And I blessed them unaware.* (286-89)

The moment he blesses the snakes, the albatross drops from his neck and sinks 'like lead into the sea' (295). Appreciating the spiritual wonder and interconnectedness of the universe and being free from negativity, the Mariner's conversion set the dead sailors' spirits free. The sailors steer the ship, which moves forward without the aid of the wind (335-40). Recognising the sacredness of the universe is the beginning of the Mariner's salvation, although he has a long way to go.

---

10. Guite, *Mariner*, p. 251.

Although the carcass is no longer hanging around his neck, the Mariner has not found absolution. As the Polar Spirit says: 'The man hath penance done, / And penance more will do' (412-13). The Polar Spirit is the spirit of the place and the guardian of the South Pole region. As a protector of nature, it seeks to avenge the killing of the albatross which it loved. However, under the influence of the angels, 'retributive vengeance is transformed into redemptive penance'.[11] The supernatural element here suggests grace as well as guilt and blame.

The arrival of the Pilot, the Pilot's boy and a Hermit links the secular and sacral world as the Mariner exclaims, 'Dear Lord in Heaven! it was a joy' (510). This phrase points to the Gospel, 'So you have pain now; but I will see you again, and your hearts will rejoice, and no one will take your joy from you' (John 16:22). The Mariner needs the assistance of the local pilot to guide his ship safely to the harbour, and the Hermit is there to help him spiritually. Thus, the Mariner seeks the Hermit to be freed from his guilt because 'He'll shrieve my soul, he'll wash away / The Albatross's blood' (516-17). The blood, in fact, has already been washed and his sin forgiven when the dead bird dropped and sank into the sea.

The Hermit asks the Mariner, 'What manner of man art thou?' (581). This question gives the Mariner the chance to confess and request penance. This thoughtless act of the Mariner has changed the course of his life and death. The bird acts as a guide to help the sailors safely navigate through the sea and poses no danger to the ship. The Mariner's penance for his cruel shooting of an innocent creature is to wander all over the world to tell the tale of his transgression and life-affirming vision.

A return to prayer liberates the Mariner from the dead albatross. Instead of having a carcass around his neck, he must now build his life around prayer, both individually and in community:

*He prayeth best, who loveth best*
*All things both great and small;*
*For the dear God who loveth us,*
*He made and loveth all* (618-21)

The Mariner realises that it is the power of prayer and love which releases him from physical and spiritual bondage. This link between prayer and love is based on the Gospel of John: 'A new commandment I

---

11. Guite, *Mariner*, p. 314.

give to you, that you love one another; even as I have loved you, that you also love one another. By this all men will know that you are my disciples, if you have love for one another' (13:34-35). From cursing God's creatures to blessing them the Mariner has come to appreciate the relation between prayer and love. As everything is linked to the web of life, all living things are to be loved and protected.

## One Life and Ecological Crisis

According to Robert Penn Warren, the main theme of *The Ancient Mariner* is the idea of 'sacramental vision' or 'One Life'.[12] The Mariner shoots the bird and suffers loneliness and spiritual agony. Recognising the beauty of the sea snakes, he experiences love which enables him to pray. Returning to his home port, the Mariner is reunited with the human community and reconciled with God.

The crew members are punished as accomplices to the crime. First, they condemn the killing because they think the bird brings good weather; then they praise the Mariner because it brings them foul weather; and when the sea is calm, they condemn him again. In other words, they see the bird merely as instrumental according to their needs. The crime of the crew members is a violation of the 'sacramental conception of the universe'. In this offence, the convenience of human beings becomes the measure of all things, thus cutting them off from nature or the 'One Life'.[13] Moores maintains that this poem is Coleridge's personal response to the 'killing' of nature which leads to 'estrangement from natural human instincts' and his conception of the unity of the cosmos.[14]

This poem dealing with the death of creatures and weather change is crucial to understanding the ecological crisis that has such a detrimental effect on human existence. The emptiness of our consumerist culture is revealed by the fact that we are never contented

---

12. Robert Penn Warren, 'A Poem of Pure Imagination: An Experiment in Reading', in James D. Boulger, *Twentieth Century Interpretations of The Rime of the Ancient Mariner; a Collection of Critical Essays* (Englewood Cliffs, NJ: Prentice Hall, 1969), p. 21. See also Edward E. Bosteltter, 'The Nightmare World of *The Ancient Mariner*' (1962) in Alun R. Jones and William Tydeman, *Coleridge: The Ancient Mariner and Other Poems; a Casebook* (London: Macmillan, 1973), pp. 184–99.
13. Warren, 'Poem of Pure Imagination', p. 28.
14. Moores, 'Oh Happy Living Things', p. 227.

despite the abundance of goods we enjoy. We are all dying of thirst, as the narrator says:

> *Water, water, every where,*
> *And all the boards did shrink;*
> *Water, water, every where,*
> *Nor any drop to drink.* (119-122)

Angry at his fate, the Mariner swears at the creatures in the sea:

> *The very deep did rot: O Christ!*
> *That ever this should be!*
> *Yea, slimy things did crawl with legs*
> *Upon the slimy sea.* (123-126)

As the vessel enters the uncharted territory of the Pacific Ocean, the wind stops, followed by scorching heat and drought. Unable to speak because of thirst, the sailors hang the albatross around the Mariner's neck (141-42). The phrase 'having an Albatross around one's neck' which means a heavy burden or responsibility, has become an idiom in the English language. Substituting the Cross, the albatross takes the place of Jesus Christ, who suffered and died for us. Representing the Mariner's guilt, the albatross has also guided the ship out of the frozen sea.

As an emblem, the dead albatross hanging around the Mariner's neck represents his guilt for having betrayed the hospitality of nature, destroying the web of life, a devastating effect felt by us as our seas today are polluted by plastic bags, bottles and trash left over by our consumer society. Birds such as the albatross which fish the waters are choked with plastic flotsam.[15] As a result of swallowing this rubbish, their digestive systems have no room left for natural sustenance. With their bloated stomachs full of waste, they die amid a great quantity of plastic products. The environmental crisis we experience today results from taking an 'instrumental attitude' towards nature with its devastating effects. The dead birds on our shores reveal who we are: 'bloated with emptiness, dying of excess, visiting destruction on our fellow creatures

---

15. *Albatross*, a film by artist Chris Jordan, is a powerfully moving love story about birds on Midway Island in the Pacific (https://www.albatrossthefilm.com/).

in the pursuit of what we ourselves can only discard'.[16] Polluting our environment due to compulsive consumption, we feel the effect of original sin more acutely than ever.

## Augustinian theology

*The Ancient Mariner* can be read as an allegory of the fall and redemption of humanity. The senseless shooting of an innocent bird symbolises the original sin inherent in all of us. The Mariner's killing of the albatross can be traced to the original sin inherited from the Fall of our first parents. St Augustine influenced Coleridge's concept of original sin as the origin of moral evil, with its emphasis on depth psychology and existential philosophy. Augustine's teaching on original sin, 'the moral sentiment', is the cause of action in this poem. The murder of the albatross by the Mariner manifests the 'inherent depravity of his will'. We witness the deepening of the Mariner's enslavement to sin, which is related to his will. With the help of prevenient grace, however, he is freed from sinful bondage; as revealed by his ability to appreciate the beauty and goodness of creation. The Mariner, aided by divine grace, will eventually be freed from original sin in a life of penance and prayer.[17]

Coleridge, like Augustine, believed that the origin of moral evil is rooted in one's will. The shooting of the albatross represents the 'amoral impulse subliminally present in the human will', which is the presence of original sin in every person.[18] In other words, each of is is born a sinner with an inherent depraved will.

The shooting of the bird reminds us of Augustine's stealing of fruit in the orchard, as narrated in the *Confessions*. The moral significance of these two acts suggests the presence of original sin, which corrupts all our acts without our knowledge or choice.[19] Regarding his stealing of the pears, Augustine asserts that this seemingly childish prank has great symbolic significance as he contemplates the origin of evil. He and his friends stole the fruit, which they did not eat but threw to the pigs for fun. Besides, Augustine's father had much better fruit in his orchard. Similarly, the Mariner's wanton act has no rational basis, but the

---

16. Guite, *Mariner*, p. 196.
17. J. A. Stuart, 'The Augustinian "Cause of Action" in Coleridge's *Rime of the Ancient Mariner*', *Harvard Theological Review* 60, no. 2 (1967), p. 180.
18. Stuart, 'Cause of Action', p. 182.
19. Stuart, 'Cause of Action', p. 183.

repercussions are fatal. Inclined towards evil, the Mariner's shooting of the albatross reveals his corrupted will, which he is powerless to control. In the *Confessions* (8.5.12), Augustine uses the example of slumber to demonstrate how we are a slave of sin without being conscious of it. In the same way, the Mariner's shooting of the bird is performed unconsciously, seemingly without control.

As the spiritual principle in human beings, Augustine understands the will as 'voluntary', with the power to direct the soul towards good or evil. To will towards the good, it needs divine assistance. Left to ourselves, we are inclined towards evil. As the psalmist says, 'Indeed, I was born guilty, a sinner when my mother conceived me' (Psalm 51:5). Sin rooted in the will is thus a voluntary transgression – this is the fallen state of the will which we exercise freely.[20] The Mariner at first perceives the water snakes as slimy, indicating his own rotten nature. He is envious that the snakes should live while his sailors are dying.

In Augustinian theology, the will is powerless to free itself from the bondage of sin to which it gives birth. Similarly, Coleridge 'while holding to the doctrine of free self-determination … at the same time agreed with the oldest and soundest theology of the Christian Church [i.e. the Augustinian], in not affirming the existence of positive and efficient power in the fallen Will, either to recover itself, or to maintain itself in holiness, after recovery'.[21] Recognising that he has fallen, the Mariner also doubts if he could be saved. With prevenient grace, as taught by Augustine, the 'kind saint' (290) can help him break out of his scepticism.

To be forgiven, the Mariner must perform 'the penance of life' for the remission of his sin. This means making people aware of the presence of original sin through the sharing of his experience and knowledge, accompanied by prayer and fellowship of the kirk. The contrast between the Mariner's joy in God's mercy and the noisy revelry of the marriage feast symbolises the sacred and the secular cities in Augustine theology. The Earthly City stands in danger of being 'unmindful of the agonizing confrontation with original sin to which God may call the individual soul without warning'.[22] In fact, this is the moral tale the Mariner feels compelled to tell the Wedding-Guest, which will make him a serious and wiser person.

---

20. Stuart, 'Cause of Action', p. 184.
21. Quoted in Stuart, 'Cause of Action', p. 186.
22. Stuart, 'Cause of Action', p. 200.

The theme of forgiveness is pivotal in the poem. In his suffering, the Mariner has time to reflect on his transgression, repent, accept responsibilities and perform penance for killing an innocent creature. Experiencing nature's backlash, he realises the importance of protecting the environment, which is part of our human existence. The health and protection of our environment are fundamental and critical to our well-being and survival. When the crew are cursed, and the ship gets stuck, the Mariner realises that it is fatal to mess with nature. The gifts of nature, such as the albatross, should be loved and cherished rather than destroyed. Feeling remorse for his impulsive act, he seeks forgiveness from his dead companions and the Hermit. When the Mariner accepts his wrongdoing, he begins to forgive himself and receive forgiveness from others.

## Monotheism and Scientific Revolution

Carl Jung holds that 'for the first time since the dawn of history we have succeeded in swallowing the whole of primitive animism into ourselves, and with it the spirit that animated nature … Now, for the first time, we are living in a lifeless nature bereft of gods.'[23] Monotheism, which suppresses the old deities, leads to the destruction of nature. The disenchanted Western mind which demystifies faith leads to the disappearance of the spirits of nature. The danger in such advancement is that we become alienated from our basic instinct that lies underneath the veneer of our so-called 'civilized values'.[24]

Scientific revolution coupled with monotheistic faith contributes greatly to the objectification of nature. Our understanding of nature 'can be seen as a projection of human perceptions of self and society onto the cosmos'.[25] In the poem, Coleridge dramatises his opposition to a mechanistic and instrumental view of nature, with the Mariner representing the European destroying nature.[26] In the Romantic tradition, Coleridge holds a unified understanding of the universe. *The Ancient Mariner* is Coleridge's attempt to embrace an organic conception of the cosmos threatened by a scientific and mechanistic worldview.

The suppression of paganism with its worship of nature and fertility cult in the Christian West has led to the demonisation of nature deities.

---

23. Quoted in Moores, 'Oh Happy Living Things', p. 229.
24. Moores, 'Oh Happy Living Things', p. 229.
25. Quoted in Moores, 'Oh Happy Living Things', p. 231.
26. Moores, 'Oh Happy Living Things', p. 231.

It is no coincidence to see the devil portrayed like a goat with horns and tail, reminiscent of the pagan worship of Pan and Dionysus. According to Jung, the sin of Satan is disobedience – representing the repressed, rebellious other-nature of European society.[27] Killing a helpful and innocent bird may also mean disobedience to one's basic instinct. The Mariner's action represents Western exploitation of the natural world, leading to isolation and alienation in the individual. Estranged from the natural world, with his deities destroyed by monotheistic tradition, the individual is lost because his human instincts are at odds with worshipping just one God.[28]

Critical of a strictly monotheistic religion with its call to subdue nature, Coleridge is more of a trinitarian theologian with Catholic sensibilities. In contrast to monotheism,

> polytheism is actually a complex and complicated system of belief that seeks to balance between natural and supernatural elements. The old religions of China and India (Hinduism) possess 'ecological wisdom' and are steeped in 'cosmic mysticism'. Monotheism, with its history of domination of nature and discrimination of women, can hardly be regarded as superior to these so-called 'primitive religions'.[29]

A trinitarian understanding of divinity strikes a good balance between monotheism's absolutism and polytheism's pluralism.

Thus, despite his belief in Christianity as a superior faith, Coleridge had conflicting views regarding monotheism as he attempted to grapple with the problem of evil. The Mariner's blessing of the water snakes, which initiates his 'psychic recovery' and redemption seems to go against the teaching of Christianity in which the serpent is demonised. Blessing the snakes 'unaware' (291) seems to imply that he is performing an act that goes against his religious belief.[30] It appears that the repressed feeling of love for creation gushes out of the deepest depth of his being, and he can even hear the sky-lark sing (363).This reading of *The Ancient Mariner* suggests that the Mariner represents the Western individual. The domination of monotheistic belief in Europe during Coleridge's

---

27. Moores, 'Oh Happy Living Things', p. 232.
28. Moores, 'Oh Happy Living Things', p. 234.
29. Ambrose Mong, *Christianity in the Modern World: A Study of Religion in a Pluralistic Society* (Cambridge: James Clarke & Co., 2021), p. 24.
30. Moores, 'Oh Happy Living Things', p. 240.

time implies that he continues to commit sin against nature which cannot be entirely absolved.[31] Perhaps some superstitious beliefs might have spurred him to care for God's creation.

## Superstition and Divine Intervention

In his lecture on 'Revealed Religion' (1795), Coleridge points out that man in his encounter with nature is tempted by superstitious belief. In 'The Destiny of Nations', Coleridge writes:

> *For Fancy is the power*
> *That first unsensualizes the dark mind,*
> *Giving it new delights; and bids it swell*
> *With wild activity; and peopling air,*
> *By obscure fears of beings in visible,*
> *Emancipates it from the grosser thrall*
> *Of the present impulse, teaching self-control,*
> *Till Superstition with unconscious hand*
> *Seat Reason on her throne.*[32]

Coleridge proposes that there are three stages in human growth: 'ignorance, superstition, and reason'. Superstition is the intermediary stage between darkness and light, as it were. Associating the albatross with divine forces in nature may indicate that the Mariner has arrived at the stage of reason, while shooting the albatross may signify suppressing the superstitious image of being rational. It can also mean retreating to ignorance: 'a relapse into his former world of fear and darkness'.[33] The negative consequences of the deed in the Mariner's mind, the feeling of guilt and remorse, indicate that he has fallen into the darkness of sin.

Atheism is related to scepticism or rejection of superstitious beliefs. John Henry Newman maintained that the superstition of simple people might be better than the scepticism of the educated. Newman feared more the danger of unbelief than that of superstition: 'I will not shrink from uttering my firm conviction, that it would be a gain to this country, were it vastly more superstitious, more bigoted, more gloomy,

---

31. Moores, 'Oh Happy Living Things', p. 243.
32. Samuel Taylor Coleridge, 'The Destiny of Nations. A Vision', https://internetpoem.com/samuel-taylor-coleridge/the-destiny-of-nations-a-vision-poem/.
33. Rookmaaker, *Romantic Conception of Nature*, p. 76.

more fierce in its religion, than at present it shows itself to be.'[34] Due to the weakness of human nature, Newman believed a little superstition could actually be the beginning of true faith. He was convinced that to be contemptuous of superstition is to be contemptuous of religion as such.[35]

Newman even considers superstition as 'man's truest and best religion, *before* the Gospel shines on him'. And thus,

> to be superstitious, – is nature's best offering, her most acceptable service, her most mature and enlarged wisdom, in the presence of a holy and offended God. They who are not superstitious without the Gospel, will not be religious with it: and I would that even in us, who have the Gospel, there were more of superstition than there is.[36]

The fear of God is the beginning of wisdom, and so is a little superstition. He writes:

> This is the idolatry of a refined age, in which the superstitions of barbarous times displease, in consequence of their grossness. Men congratulate themselves on their emancipation from forms and their enlightened worship, when they are but in the straight course to a worse captivity, and are exchanging dependence on the creature for dependence on self.[37]

Having rejected superstition, the Mariner enters a dead world where even the sun and moon appear threatening. Relying solely on his sense perception or 'dependence on self', he perceives nothing beyond

---

34. John Henry Newman, 'Sermon 24 – The Religion of the Day', *Newman Reader*, http://www.newmanreader.org/works/parochial/volume1/sermon24.html, 2:320. This section on superstition is taken from Ambrose Mong, *Power of Popular Piety: A Critical Examination* (Eugene, OR: Wipf & Stock Publishers, 2019), pp. 88–90.
35. Edward Short, 'John Henry Newman in the "Realms of Superstition"', *Newman Studies Journal* 12, no. 2 (2015), p. 68.
36. John Henry Newman, 'Sermon 6 – On Justice, as a Principle of Divine Governance', *Newman Reader*, http://www.newmanreader.org/works/oxford/sermon6.html, 4:18–19.
37. John Henry Newman, 'Lectures on the Doctrine of Justification', *Newman Reader*, http://www.newmanreader.org/works/justification/lecture4.html, 4:24.

himself, not even God. In fact, he is not even aware that all the horror that he experiences is a projection of his own alienated mind.[38] In other words, his sense perception becomes the criteria of truth, which is totally subjective.

The recovery process begins when the Mariner regains contact with nature and, fellow human beings and starts praying. At this moment, a 'spring of love' (288) leads to a change of heart when he blesses the water snakes unaware (291). Although the albatross drops off from his neck, the Mariner still has a long way to go: 'his future fate is to enact a process towards the cross, the stage of superstition in which life is at least bearable'.[39] However, it is doubtful that he will arrive at the stage of reason because he is unaware of what he experiences.

The Mariner's belief in divine intervention on his behalf enables him to return to nature, the community and God himself. Experiencing isolation, he realises his great need for God. The miraculous wind and the resurrection of his crew have led him to believe in divine power, even if this conviction is based on superstition. The important point is that he is no longer alienated from God and men.[40] This is revealed by his worship of God in community (610).

In contrast to the superstition of the Pilot and the Pilot's boy, 'we hear the accents of religion modulated and enriched by admiration of the natural world' in the Hermit's voice.[41] In the poem, the Hermit is the first to hear the Mariner's tale. The unfolding stages of the narration and the intellectual complexities of the poem imposed by Coleridge in his successive revisions suggest a 'quasi-Hegelian history' of the 'more philosophical phases of Christianity'.[42] *The Ancient Mariner* thus can be interpreted as the Christian story of sin and salvation, the redemption of creation, human beings and nature. Traumatised by survivor guilt, the Mariner seeks forgiveness, absolution and penance.

---

38. Rookmaaker, *Romantic Conception of Nature*, p. 77.
39. Rookmaaker, *Romantic Conception of Nature*, p. 79.
40. Rookmaaker, *Romantic Conception of Nature*, p. 83.
41. Paul H. Fry, 'Biographical and Historical Contexts', in Coleridge and Fry, *The Rime of the Ancient Mariner*, p. 17.
42. Fry, 'Biographical and Historical Contexts', p. 19. See also Jack Stillinger, 'The Multiple Versions of Coleridge's Poems: How Many "Mariners" Did Coleridge Write?', *Studies in Romanticism* 31, no. 2 (1992), pp. 127–46.

## Conversion

For Coleridge, knowledge such as history, philosophy, poetry and science reveals the truth of Christianity. The whole created order is fulfilled and perfected in the person of Christ. Not based on blind faith, he subjected his religious conviction to scientific and philosophical examination. Central to *The Ancient Mariner* is the theme of self-inflicted alienation that separates human beings from the rest of creation. Nonetheless, the fragmented creation can be restored through a spiritual conversion when the Mariner eventually returns to his true home. This idea of a shattered universe made whole through the fall and redemption of human beings is a constant theme reflected in Coleridge's intellectual and spiritual life.[43]

Coleridge believes that our broken humanity, the result of the erosion of morality and intellect, could be restored by submitting our will to God. His desire for unity is expressed in pantheistic terms – the universal Spirit.[44] In other words, God's presence is everywhere; he is both immanent and transcendent. Coleridge also identifies the principles of 'Being' (Intellect and Action) with the trinitarian God, which is the general basis of all knowledge. In his mature years, Coleridge rejected Christian sects such as Unitarianism and Socinianism that deny the triune God, asserting that the Trinity is the only satisfactory symbol of ultimate reality: 'the primary Idea, out of which all other ideas are evolved … the Mystery (Idea) in which are hidden all the Treasures of knowledge'.[45] This trinitarian image is also present in the way the three legitimate siblings relate to one another in Fyodor Dostoevsky's novel, *The Brothers Karamazov*.

---

43. Mary Anne Perkins, 'Religious Thinker', in Newlyn, *Cambridge Companion to Coleridge*, p. 188. See also J. Robert Barth, *Coleridge and Christian Doctrine* (Cambridge, MA: Harvard University Press, 1969), pp. 85–104.
44. Perkins, 'Religious Thinker', p. 188.
45. Quoted in Perkins, 'Religious Thinker', p. 189.

# Chapter 6

# *The Brothers Karamazov*

## Fyodor Dostoevsky (1821-1881)

The novelist Fyodor Dostoevsky was born in Moscow and died in St Peterburg, Russia. In his writings, Dostoevsky conveys abstract and complex Christian doctrine that is meaningful and poignant. However, his religious ideas are rooted in the world, unconcerned with abstract theology. In his literary technique, Dostoevsky presents multiple voices, both opposing and equally privileged. Mikhail Bakhtin characterised Dostoevsky's work as 'polyphonic':

> A character's word about himself and his world is just as fully weighted as the author's word usually is; it is not subordinated to the character's objectified image as merely one of his characteristics, nor does it serve as a mouthpiece for the author's voice. It possesses extraordinary independence in the structure of the work; it sounds, as it were, alongside the author's word and in a special way combines both with it and with the full and equally valid voices of other characters.[1]

Thus, instead of a single narrator's voice, a plurality of consciousness, each with its own perspective, is put forward. It is no wonder that

---

1. Mikhail Bakhtin, *Problems of Dostoevsky's Poetics,* ed. Caryl Emerson (Minneapolis: University of Minnesota Press, 1984), p. 7.

the works of Dostoevsky are subjected to diverse interpretations in philosophy, theology and psychology. Indeed, Dostoevsky's writings have exerted a profound influence on modern Western thought.

In his early life, besides suffering from an epileptic fit, Dostoevsky was imprisoned in Siberia from 1850 to 1854, and he was able to create his characters by drawing on dramatic prison incidents, personal experiences and his family life. Dostoevsky was raised in the traditional piety of the Orthodox Church; his father was a doctor working in the hospital for the poor in Moscow, and his mother was a cultured and caring woman. Following his father's advice, Dostoevsky was enrolled in the Academy of Military Engineering in St Petersburg, although he was ill-suited for that kind of life. Nevertheless, he graduated from the Military Academy and served as a sublieutenant, but eventually resigned to become a writer.

## Political Conviction and Faith

Dostoevsky participated in the Petrashevsky Circle, a group of progressive Russian intellectuals whose leader was M. V. Petrahevsky (1821-66). He was arrested on 23 April 1849 together with other members. The Tsarist government of Nicolas I condemned the liberal and republican ideas of the Circle and sentenced the 21 of them to death 'for plotting the overthrow of the existing … laws and system of government'.[2] However, on the day of execution, the death sentence was commuted to hard labour in Siberia. Being spared from execution led Dostoevsky to appreciate life as a gift and value freedom, integrity and individual responsibility. During his four years in prison, Dostoevsky experienced a 'regeneration' of his faith;[3] suffering in Siberia strengthened his Christian conviction, especially when it brought him face to face with evil.

Embracing Russian Orthodoxy as the people's faith, Dostoevsky fought against the scepticism and materialism of the West. His religious belief influenced his post-Siberian writings. His narratives are charged with religious or biblical imagery within a redemptive structure. His novels attempt to confront believers and unbelievers on equal terms.

---

2. N. Troyan, 'The Philosophical Opinions of the Petrashevsky Circle', *Philosophy and Phenomenological Research* 6, no. 3 (1946), p. 363.

3. Gary Saul Morson, 'Fyodor Dostoyevsky', *Encyclopedia Britannica*, 7 November 2022, https://www.britannica.com/biography/Fyodor-Dostoyevsky.

Religious themes dominate *The Brothers Karamazov* more than they do other works by Dostoevsky. When writing this novel, Dostoevsky was firmly committed to his Christian belief and wanted to share his faith. He believes Christianity is not just an ideal but a vivid reality, a refuge for Russians against evil. He portrays Christianity in the Orthodox way:

> a remarkable and theologically consistent tradition, which includes the Greek Fathers of the fourth century, the Christology of Cyril of Alexandria, and the synthesis of Maximus the Confessor and of Gregory Palamas ... the mainstream of theological thought in Byzantium ... [which] ... coincides with the very content of Orthodox religious experience.[4]

In this chapter on *The Brothers Karamazov*, we will explore Dostoevsky's characterisation of good and evil and debate on the existence of God. In addition to the author's criticism of Catholicism and his support for the Orthodox theory of *sorbornost*, we conclude the chapter with an examination of the trinitarian image.

## A Tragedy

*The Brothers Karamazov*, Dostoevsky's last and most significant work, deals with theological and philosophical themes. This gripping story recounts a tragedy involving four brothers – Dmitri, Ivan, Alyosha, the illegitimate Smerdyako – and the murder of their father, Fyodor.

A buffoon and debauched character, Fyodor ridicules all that is noble and decent whenever the opportunity arises. Neglecting his children from his two wives, he left them to the care of his servants. Dmitri, the eldest son from his first wife Adelaide Ivanovna Miusov, is a passionate and sincere character who fights with his father over money and a woman. The other two legitimate sons from Fyodor's second wife, Sofia Ivanova, are Ivan, an intellectual and free thinker, and Alyosha, a novice monk who attempts to put Christian love into practice. The main concern in this novel is what Ivan calls 'eternal questions, of the existence of God

---

4. Quoted in Oral John Marrs, 'Of "Minimal Religion," a Mystical Discourse on Orthodox Spirituality in the Life, Discourses, and Sermons of Father Zosima, in Book Six of the Brothers Karamazov', *St Vladimir's Theological Quarterly* 61, no. 4 (2017), p. 426.

and immortality'.[5] The story's stage is set when Dmitri says, 'God and the devil are fighting there and the battlefield is the heart of man.'[6]

The story begins with the son and father, Dmitri and Fyodor, fighting over money and a beautiful woman, Grushenka. Complicating this love triangle is another woman, Katerina Ivanovna, who is engaged to Dmitri. The first major scene takes place when the family assembles in a monastic cell, in the presence of Father Zosima, attempting to reconcile Dmitri and his father. Zosima is an elderly priest and mentor to Alyosha. The meeting breaks down when Fyodor makes a fool of himself and offends the monks, which only increases Dimitri's hatred towards his father. In spite of this fiasco, this scene conveys much of Ivan's outlook regarding God's existence and the soul's immortality. In the conversation between Ivan and Alyosha, Dostoevsky discusses Ivan's moral standpoint, which culminates in 'The Grand Inquisitor'.

Following Ivan's prose poem, 'The Grand Inquisitor', is the deathbed scene of Father Zosima, when he narrates the story of his life to Alyosha, including his elder brother's remarkable conversion. Influenced by his brother Markel, Zosima's belief, which Alyosha upholds, is that we have sinned and are responsible for everyone and everything. After the death of Father Zosima, Alyosha undergoes an intense spiritual crisis.

In the meantime, Dmitri desperately tries to raise 3,000 roubles to start a new life with Grushenka. Later, one night Dmitri visits Grushenka with a roll of banknotes. When Fyodor Karamazov is found dead, all the evidence points to Dmitri as the murderer. Dmitri admits that he has attacked an old servant who caught him fleeing his father's house but insists on his innocence.

In the days preceding the court trial, we witness Alyosha getting involved with a disabled young girl, Lisa Hohlakov, and meeting an extraordinary group of boys. While protesting his innocence, Dmitri experiences a profound spiritual transformation. He is no longer afraid of punishment as Grushenka promises to be with him even in Siberia. Sharing the same belief as Father Zosima and Alyosha, Dmitri says, 'we are all responsible for all … I go for all, because someone must go for all. I didn't kill father, but I've got to go. I accept it.'[7]

Ivan, too, undergoes a profound experience. Half convinced that Smerdyakov killed his father, he feels responsible for this crime as he

---

5. Fyodor Dostoevsky, *The Brothers Karamazov: The Constance Garnett Translation Revised by Ralph E. Matlaw* (New York: Norton, 1976), p. 215.
6. Dostoevsky, *The Brothers Karamazov*, p. 97.
7. Dostoevsky, *The Brothers Karamazov*, p. 560.

had spent much time discussing social theories with this half-brother. Smerdyakov has been emboldened by Ivan's idea that everything is permitted, including murder. After three interviews before Dmitri's trial, Smerdyakov admits his guilt and makes it clear that Ivan's ethical viewpoint inspired him.

Feeling guilty and remorseful, Ivan encounters the devil in a nightmarish hallucination. This hellish vision ends with the appearance of Alyosha. Ivan falls into a fever and resolves to reveal Symerdyakov's and his own guilt at the trial of Dmitri the following day. However, Ivan's testimony is dismissed during the trial due to a lack of evidence and his deranged mental condition. Further, Katrina produces a damning letter that Dmitri wrote to her about how he would kill his father. The defence attorney's eloquent argument fails to convince the jury. Found guilty, Dmitri is sentenced to exile in Siberia.

The novel ends with Katrina, having undergone a change of heart, attempting to arrange with Ivan for Dmitri's escape with Grushenka. Unfortunately, by this time, Ivan has suffered an almost complete mental breakdown. Only Alyosha remains calm with a heart full of compassion, exhorting the children he has met earlier to be kind and honest. He tells them not to be afraid of life and reminds them of the resurrection when they will meet each other again in joy. The boys respond – 'Hurrah for Karamazov.'[8]

## Good and Evil

In this novel, the characters display much ambiguity and dualism around the presence of good and evil. We witness humility and pride, love and loathing, kindness and cruelty. Reality is also elusive, especially when evil can lead to damnation or salvation, despair or hope, and ideas can be divine or devilish. 'Beauty is a riddle' because it can captivate or liberate, passion is torn between lust and love, and freedom can be a redeeming good or an enslaving evil. God hides and reveals himself, dies and resurrects.[9] Our experience of reality is never straightforward; it is enigmatic until the final triumph of good over evil. In Dostoevsky's

---

8. Dostoevsky, *The Brothers Karamazov*, p. 735.
9. Pablo Blanco Sarto, 'Dostoevsky Overcomes Nihilism: Luigi Pareyson Reads *The Brothers Karamazov*', *Wrocławski Przegląd Teologiczny* 29, no. 1 (2021), p. 404. See also Dennis Vanden Auweele, 'Existential Struggles in Dostoevsky's *The Brothers Karamazov*', *International Journal for Philosophy of Religion* 80, no. 3 (2016), pp. 279–96.

characters, especially in the Karamazov brothers, we witness extreme good and evil fighting within the human heart.

The 'old buffoon' Fyodor Karamazov is an obnoxious and ridiculous fellow who tends to degrade himself in front of others. A slave to sensuality, he is vindictive and the cause of his family's misfortune. Fyodor's illegitimate son, Smerdyakov, 'carries within himself two souls: submissive to the point of subservience, but rebellious to the point of arrogance; interested in subtle, theological debates, but able to carry out the assassination of his own father with cunning and thoroughness'.[10] He is both 'the devil's son' and 'a holy innocent' as he assimilates the worst and best in his society.[11] Incarnating the worst in Ivan's character, Smerdyakov pursues his godless doctrine to its logical extreme, which is murder and suicide.

Portrayed as an evil character, Smerdyakov plays the role of Judas. For example, he refuses to take the 3,000 roubles for which he murdered Fyodor. With no recourse to spiritual guidance, he commits suicide. Like Judas, he betrays his master for money. The 3,000 roubles correspond to the biblical equivalent of thirty pieces of silver (Matt. 26:15). Later, he hangs himself in despair (Matt. 27:3-8).

Against the simplistic vision of the human being as good or innocent by nature, Dostoevsky presents to us a person capable of doing evil. Neither a Manichaean nor someone who denies the reality of evil, Dostoevsky believes evil exists and can be overcome by good. His philosophy asserts evil is not merely the absence of good as St Augustine teaches, nor simply the product of the environment, as the determinists claim. It does not come from an evil deity, 'a principle that is opposed to God', as the Manichaeans maintain. Evil, according to Dostoevsky, 'is a *rebellious* principle against the Absolute Being, against the Infinite Good, against God'.[12] The presence of evil is due to the freedom given to us to reject what is good. Its origin is rebellion and pride, the desire to be like gods.

At the other end of the spectrum is Father Zosima, the personification of good – a reference point for all that is holy and virtuous. His response

---

10. Sarto, 'Dostoevsky Overcomes Nihilism', p. 408.
11. Sharon Cohen, '"Balaam's Ass": Smerdyakov as a Paradoxical Redeemer in Dostoevsky's *The Brothers Karamazov*', *Christianity and Literature* 64, no. 1 (2014), p. 46. See also Marina Kanevskaya, 'Smerdiakov and Ivan: Dostoevsky's *The Brothers Karamazov*', *The Russian Review* (Stanford) 61, no. 3 (2002), pp. 358–76.
12. Quoted in Sarto, 'Dostoevsky Overcomes Nihilism', p. 401.

to Ivan's atheism is a love that goes beyond pain and suffering. Like Christ, the saintly Zosima maintains his silence in the face of Ivan's atheistic belief as a kind of rebuttal. Zosima, however, performs an act of reverence before Dmitri: he 'moved towards Dmitri Fydorovich and reaching him sank on his knees before him. Alyosha thought he had fallen from weakness, but this was not so. The elder distinctly and deliberately bowed down at Dmitri Fydorovich's feet till his forehead touched the floor.'[13] This foreshadows the sacrifice Dmitri will undertake when he willingly accepts the punishment for a crime he did not commit.

Evil is destroyed when good triumphs: 'evil turns into good, death into life, the negative into the positive, destruction into construction'. Evil can have a positive effect when it raises a person to a higher moral level. Thus, 'the true good is not the innocence of having no knowledge of sin, but the virtue that is the victory over sin'. The transformation of evil into good takes place in the presence of *pain*. 'Evil has a positive value, in that, through pain, it turns into a proclamation of good.'[14] Through the experience of pain, the person encounters a crisis which can turn evil into good. In other words, through repentance, pain can be transformed into joy.

Given the above reflection, we witness Dmitri Karamazov as the character who truly personifies within himself the battle between good and evil, the tragic condition of humanity, the fall and redemption of humanity, 'a synthesis of sin and faith'.[15] A hot-tempered and brutal character, he also possesses a certain nobleness and magnanimity in the way he loves Grushenka. Indeed, Dmitri is a complex character: 'He falls into the abyss of evil and lust like his father, but he also possesses the capacity for intellectual elevation like Ivan, and the capacity for reaching mystical heights like Alyosha.'[16]

Dmitri and Ivan share the same concern for the suffering of innocent children. But it is Dmitri who can resolve this problem of suffering when he accepts his unjust punishment, taking responsibility for the woes of the world. Transformed into a 'new man', Dmitri finds happiness and love as he prepares for exile in Siberia. Only with the 'dialectic of freedom', involving suffering and pain, which Dmitri attains, can human beings experience inner liberation and survive the nihilism of Siberia. This was what happened to Dostoevsky when he was sentenced to forced

---

13. Dostoevsky, *The Brothers Karamazov*, p. 65.
14. Quoted in Sarto, 'Dostoevsky Overcomes Nihilism', p. 402.
15. Sarto, 'Dostoevsky Overcomes Nihilism', p. 409.
16. Quoted in Sarto, 'Dostoevsky Overcomes Nihilism', p. 409.

labour – the experience transformed him spiritually. He confessed how he was saved from sinking into depression and despair (like descending into hell) by reading a small copy of the Bible hidden under his pillow.[17]

The remaining Karamazov, Alyosha, is an 'angel' with a tolerant and compassionate nature. He is the only one in the family who accepts the old Karamazov as he is – a failed father. A sensitive young man, he represents the holy and innocent. Alyosha accepts Ivan's criticism of Christianity with a silence similar to that of his spiritual director, Father Zosima. In response to Ivan's doubt about the purpose of suffering, Alyosha stresses the scandal of the cross, the death and resurrection of Jesus. Attempting to refute Ivan's atheism, Alyosha says 'there is a Being and He can forgive everything, all and *for all*, because He gave His innocent blood for all and everything'.[18] Alyosha believes there is forgiveness, even for those who torture children, because no one is beyond redemption. Through this novice monk, Dostoevsky teaches that we all have the responsibility to abolish suffering.

An intellectual, Ivan claims that everything is permitted, but he does not act on his belief at the moment of reckoning. Ivan's atheism is the consequence of not being able to accept the suffering of innocent children – it is the atheism of empathy for the pain of others and indignation at such an indifferent deity. According to Ivan, a God who permits this kind of evil does not exist. If God or immortality does not exist, then 'everything would be lawful, even cannibalism'.[19] The bastard, Smerdyakov, carries out what Ivan insinuates, parricide. Upon witnessing the tragic consequences of his godless ideology, Ivan suffers a mental derangement.

## Existence of God

According to A. Gibson, Ivan is not an atheist but rather an 'anti-theist', in that he does not deny the existence of God but defies him.[20] Ivan merely asks, 'why should the innocent suffer'? As we shall see later, Ivan is a sincere man with a conscience, as evidenced by his attempt to save Dmitri from being falsely convicted for killing their father. He even

---

17. Sarto, 'Dostoevsky Overcomes Nihilism', p. 410.
18. Dostoevsky, *The Brothers Karamazov*, pp. 226–27.
19. Dostoevsky, *The Brothers Karamazov*, p. 60.
20. A. Boyce Gibson, *The Religion of Dostoevsky* (Philadelphia, PA: Westminster Press, 1973), p. 179.

takes the blame for the death of their father. Thus, the portrayal of Ivan as an atheist by Dostoevsky appears contradictory.

The setting for Dostoevsky's discussion on the existence of God takes place in a tavern. Ivan advises Alyosha not to think about whether God exists because such questions are beyond human comprehension. Yet Ivan says: 'I accept God and am glad to, and what's more, I accept His wisdom, His purpose.'[21] But he does not and cannot accept the world that God created. Ivan's atheism is thus a qualified one.

There is also a trivial discussion among the boys in the tavern regarding God and immortality: 'most original Russian boys do nothing but talk of the eternal questions'.[22] Such questions are, in fact, not frivolous; Kant has shown that certain disputes cannot be resolved, and must sometimes be presented in such a way that no answer is possible. Kant 'found it necessary to deny knowledge [of transcendent realities such as God] in order to make room for faith'.[23]

In response to the Russian boys' attempt to justify the ways of God to man, Ivan asserts: 'I understand nothing ... I don't want to understand anything now. I want to stick to the fact. I made up my mind long ago not to understand. If I try to understand anything, I shall be false to the fact, and I have determined to stick to the fact.'[24] He also provides Alyosha with an alternative answer: 'I am trying to explain as quickly as possible my essential nature, that is what manner of man I am, what I believe in, and for what I hope, that's it, isn't it?'[25] Dostoevsky is not presenting a dispute between the existence and non-existence of God, but Ivan's rejection of the world that God has created.

Ivan's atheism is a moral response to the Christian understanding of creation, which he rejects. The sufferings of innocent children and their extreme cruelty demonstrate the contradiction between a loving God and our world. The Christian understanding of the existence of evil, theodicy, fails to satisfy Ivan because it goes against facts: 'Listen! If all must suffer to pay for the eternal harmony, what have children to do with it, tell me, please? It's beyond all comprehension why they should

---

21. Dostoevsky, *The Brothers Karamazov*, p. 216.
22. Dostoevsky, *The Brothers Karamazov*, p. 215.
23. Quoted in R. Maurice Barineau, 'The Triumph of Ethics over Doubt: Dostoevsky's *The Brothers Karamazov*', *Christianity and Literature* 43, no. 3/4 (1994), p. 388.
24. Dostoevsky, *The Brothers Karamazov*, p. 224.
25. Dostoevsky, *The Brothers Karamazov*, p. 216.

suffer, and why they should pay for the harmony. Why should they, too, furnish material to enrich the soil for the harmony of the future?'[26]

The discussion regarding the existence of God cannot be based on speculation about the motivation of an omnipotent deity who is supposed to be loved. The presence of evil and suffering in the world contradicts this belief. Facts can be used to prove that God does not exist, although Ivan denies such a possibility when he says: 'I have a Euclidian earthly mind, and how could I solve problems that are not of this world?'[27] His protest against God is fundamentally 'in the name of morality' rather than in epistemological terms.[28] Further, he rejects any theory regarding the defence of God in the face of evil or theodicy. In his response to the realities of suffering, the focus is on creation rather than the creator. Alyosha calls Ivan's response a 'rebellion'. Ivan replies: 'Rebellion? I am sorry you call it that … One can hardly live in rebellion, and I want to live.'[29] Ivan thus refuses to enter paradise because the price is the suffering of innocent people and he hastens to return the entrance ticket.

The God that Ivan acknowledges is a 'false God', one invented by humans through speculation; Ivan is, in fact, 'accepting and projecting the trivialization of the concept of God'; his atheism is thus 'profoundly and intentionally blasphemous'.[30] Albert Camus writes:

> Ivan explicitly rejects the mystery and, consequently, God, on the principle of love … Ivan rejects the basic interdependence, introduced by Christianity, between suffering and truth. Ivan's most profound utterance, the one which opens the deepest chasms beneath the rebel's feet, is his even if: 'I would persist in my indignation *even if* I were wrong' … Ivan incarnates the refusal of salvation. Faith leads to immortal life. But faith presumes the acceptance of the mystery and of evil, and resignation to injustice.[31]

---

26. Dostoevsky, *The Brothers Karamazov*, p. 225.
27. Dostoevsky, *The Brothers Karamazov*, p. 216.
28. Stewart R. Sutherland, *Atheism and the Rejection of God: Contemporary Philosophy and The Brothers Karamazov* (Oxford: Blackwell, 1977), p. 30.
29. Dostoevsky, *The Brothers Karamazov*, p. 226.
30. Sutherland, *Atheism and the Rejection of God*, pp. 31, 33.
31. Albert Camus, *The Rebel: An Essay on Man in Revolt* (New York: Vintage, 1991), https://search-ebscohost com.easyaccess1.lib.cuhk.edu.hk/login.aspx?direct=true&db=nlebk&AN=733722&site=ehost-live&scope=site.

Thus, even if there is a relationship between suffering and truth, Ivan the rebel will continue to hold steadfast to his free-thinking because he cannot accept a God who allows the suffering of innocent children. He sees no purpose in their senseless pain. It is simply 'too high a price to pay for the sake of harmony'.[32] For Ivan, suffering can never be seen as a means to a higher purpose. Nothing can ever compensate for the suffering of the innocent. Thus, his rebellion includes the denial of the concept of God, and all that goes with it, such as prayer, worship, miracles, immortality and eternal life. However, Ivan accepts a finite god, the product of a Euclidean mind, one we can think and talk about in 'anthropomorphic terms'.[33] The proposition 'God exists' is related to the difference between belief and unbelief and the way we live our life based on that distinction.

Ivan's atheism allows for the existence of God but not the justification of God's creation. No restitution is possible in such an unjust world filled with abuses. The ultimate reconciliation in the fullness of time cannot compensate for the suffering of innocent children and the horrible injustice suffered by people throughout history. Like the Grand Inquisitor, Ivan does not believe in God nor in man and his freedom, although he loves humanity. The conversation between Ivan and Alyosha regarding the existence of God and suffering provides the context for the Legend of the Grand Inquisitor.

## The Grand Inquisitor

This prose poem, narrated by Ivan, tells how Jesus returns to the world in Seville in the sixteenth century after the successful burning of heretics by the Spanish Inquisition. Jesus performs the usual miracles, such as curing the blind and raising the dead, and is warmly welcomed by the people. Despite his good works, he is arrested and put in prison by the Grand Inquisitor. Visiting Jesus secretly at night, the Grand Inquisitor explains to Jesus that human beings are naturally rebellious and need to be controlled. Rebels are naturally discontented; giving them freedom will only lead to greater dissatisfaction.

Be that as it may, when Jesus was tempted in the wilderness for the sake of freedom, he rejected three things that people persistently pursue: bread, power and worldly recognition. For Dostoevsky, the experience of God is related to the freedom to choose between good

---

32. Dostoevsky, *The Brothers Karamazov*, p. 226.
33. Sutherland, *Atheism and the Rejection of God*, p. 36.

and evil, obedience and rebellion. The Church, however, curtails this freedom and convinces the faithful to believe in 'mystery, miracle and authority'.[34] For the sake of the happiness of the majority of people who cannot cope with any freedom, the Church replaces Christ's freedom with its organisation. Being the Son of God and living in spiritual splendour, Christ's standard is too high for most believers. Thus, the Grand Inquisitor tells Christ that he is not allowed to continue his ministry on earth because his work contradicts the mission of the Church. By rejecting the three temptations, Christ has guaranteed free will to human beings, yet free will is an unbearable burden for humanity. Christ gives people the freedom to follow him, 'the fearful burden of free choice',[35] yet many are not strong enough to carry that weight.

The Grand Inquisitor insists that Christ should give people no choice and thus remove the burden of decision from their shoulders. That is to say, instead of freedom, Christ should offer security. In this way, people who are too weak to follow him and may not be saved will at least have some security and happiness on earth. Moral freedom is an impossible burden, the Grand Inquisitor insists. The Church must correct the mistake of Christ by taking away the freedom of choice and replacing it with security. The Grand Inquisitor must keep Christ in prison because, if Christ is allowed to be free, he would undermine the Church's mission to lift the burden of free will from humankind. In fact, the Grand Inquisitor threatens to burn Jesus like the rest of the heretics. In the end, Christ answers the Grand Inquisitor by kissing him on his bloodless lip. Still adhering to his idea, the Grand Inquisitor opens the prison door and says to Christ: 'Go, and come no more ... come not at all, never, never!'[36] The Church remains irreconcilable with the vision of Christ.

As the narrator of this story, Ivan seems to identify with the Grand Inquisitor's Christian faith, but Christ's compassion moved him. The kiss given by Christ to the Grand Inquisitor highlights the importance of peace and forgiveness. This story undermines Ivan's insistence that 'all is permitted', which is replaced by 'all is controlled' to avert unhappiness from humanity. Dostoevsky maintained that the desire for absolute control in both the sacred and spiritual spheres characterised the Catholic Church.

---

34. Dostoevsky, *The Brothers Karamazov*, p. 236.
35. Dostoevsky, *The Brothers Karamazov*, p. 235.
36. Dostoevsky, *The Brothers Karamazov*, p. 243.

## Catholicism and Socialism

In 'The Grand Inquisitor' Dostoevsky attempts to expose the evils of Roman Catholicism and socialism. He had flirted with socialism in his younger days. As mentioned earlier, the years of hardship and suffering in Siberia had a profound effect on Dostoevsky which served to bring out his spiritual side. He endured his punishment in prison without anger or bitterness but emerged out of it as a devout Christian. Experiencing a rebirth, he developed a love for the Scriptures and a personal attachment to Christ in the Gospel. In a letter from prison in 1854, he professed: 'If anyone could prove to me that Christ is outside the truth, and if the truth really did exclude Christ, I would prefer to stay with Christ and not with the truth.'[37]

While in prison, Dostoevsky contemplated the conflict between the irrational and rational faculties. He prefers the love of Christ to the logic of the Grand Inquisitor. The Inquisitor's ideology is based on a rational system of law and order imposed on the faithful by means of 'miracle, mystery, and authority'.[38] Like the socialists in Europe, the Grand Inquisitor rejects the truth which is Christ and establishes a Church that is authoritarian and oppressive. On the other hand, Christ offers people freedom and love unconditionally. Dostoevsky alleged that Roman Catholicism had betrayed the teaching of Christ in favour of despotism. Catholicism, like socialism, demands the total submission of its adherents, renunciation of their freedom, a fidelity based on fear rather than on love.[39] This is exactly what the Grand Inquisitor requires of the believers.

The Grand Inquisitor represents what Romano Guardini calls 'Ecclesiasticism', a system that guarantees salvation merely by following the Church's command.[40] Such a system replaces grace and freedom with laws and domination. This contradicts the true spirit of Christianity, which emphasises humanity's relationship with God. Dostoevsky condemned the Catholic Church for such practices, which go against Christianity's true spirit. Guardini acknowledges that there might be some truth in this accusation in spite of the author's misrepresentation.

---

37. Quoted in Jerry S. Wasserman, 'Introduction', in Fyodor Dostoyevsky, *The Grand Inquisitor*, ed. Jerry S. Wasserman (Columbus, OH: Charles E. Merrill Pub. Co., 1970), p. 6.
38. Dostoevsky, *The Brothers Karamazov*, p. 236.
39. Wasserman, 'Introduction', in Dostoyevsky, *The Grand Inquisitor*, p. 7.
40. Romano Guardini, 'The Legend of the Grand Inquisitor', *Cross Current* 3, no. 1 (1952), p. 61.

Dostoevsky also accused the Catholic Church of using force and power to achieve unity. It seeks to subjugate its believers in the name of Christ. Interfering with politics, the Catholic Church, with its 'subtle' and 'calculating propaganda', appears like a secular movement under the show of spirituality, according to Dostoevsky. From the Orthodox Church's point of view, the Catholic Church practised 'casuistry' and 'compromise' through controlling believers. Not embodying the Spirit of Church, it was the Church of Reason and Matter.[41] In the nineteenth century, despite its opposition towards those who violate tradition, faith and morality, the Catholic Church appeared to have upheld the spirit of 'utilitarianism and materialism'. In his travels abroad (1867-71), Dostoevsky had witnessed the onslaught of 'intellectualized Westernism' and also 'secularized ecclesiasticism'.[42]

Upholding papal infallibility. which was declared during the First Vatican Council (1869-70), and Ultramontanism, a doctrine that supports supreme papal authority, the Catholic Church appeared to Dostoevsky to have mixed the interests of the Church with those of the State. Further, by proclaiming papal infallibility, the Catholic Church came into direct conflict with the Orthodox Church which declared that the decision of the first seven Church Councils is the only valid and unalterable definition of Christian faith and dogma.

Dostoevsky failed to acknowledge the contributions of the Catholic Church's early fathers and mystics, saints such Ambrose, Augustine, Jerome, Benedict and Francis, who revived Christianity in difficult times. Influenced primarily by the events of his times, Dostoevsky perceived Roman Catholicism merely as a historical and political institution and a church cut off from its contemplative and mystical vocation. Though both Orthodoxy and Catholicism were critical of 'modernism', Dostoevsky complained that the Catholic Church had taken advantage of every situation to enhance its political interests, as demonstrated by its global dominance. Alarmed by the power and prestige of Roman Catholicism in the mid-nineteenth century, he held that the Catholic Church functioned more like a political power.

Dostoevsky was concerned that increasing papal power enshrined in the Catholic Church's monarchical structure would threaten the Eastern Orthodox Church in Russia. In fact, 'the great struggle between Russia and the West was, in reality, the conflict between the ascetical spirituality of the Holy Orthodox Church of the East and the ecclesiastical secularism

---

41. George A. Panichas, 'Fyodor Dostoevsky and Roman Catholicism', *Greek Orthodox Theological Review* 4, no. 1 (1958), p. 17.
42. Panichas, 'Dostoevsky and Roman Catholicism', p. 19.

of the Roman Catholic Church of the West'.[43] The promulgation of papal infallibility gave the pontiff supreme power over the Catholic Church. Fearful of being excommunicated, the Catholic bishops acted according to command rather than by conviction. When the pope declared, *La tradizione son' io* (I am the tradition), it reminds us of the Grand Inquisitor in *The Brothers Karamazov*. The pope's absolute power in faith and doctrine highlights the difference between the Western Latin Church and the Eastern Orthodox Church.

Strengthening the pope's power weakens the role of the laity. It signifies for Dostoevsky a kind of *spiritual nihilism* or 'ecclesiastical Romanism', which is no different from the Westernism that corrupts many Russians. The pontiff, proclaiming himself the Vicar of Christ on earth, will eventually replace the Lord Jesus Christ. According to Dostoevsky, Roman theology is essentially a secular teaching that emphasises the historical Jesus who had come and gone. Orthodox theology, on the other hand, stresses the spiritual Christ who is ever present in our souls.[44] Dostoevsky believed that the Orthodox Church was more concerned with the spiritual life of its believers.

Because of its involvement in politics, Dostoevsky claimed that Roman Catholicism was the cause of European materialism, atheism and socialism. Hence in Europe, we witness a deterioration, perversion, and loss of Christian principles. Underlying this grave concern was his belief in Russian political and ideological supremacy. The infiltration of Russia by the social-political philosophies of Feuerbach, Comte, Marx, Voltaire and Rousseau alarmed Dostoevsky.[45]

Comparing papal infallibility to the third temptation of the devil, to which the Catholic Church had succumbed with its global domination, Dostoevsky trusted that Russian Orthodoxy would help to restore Christianity to its purity by opposing future socialism.[46] In *The Brothers Karamazov*, Father Paissy says:

> Understand the Church is not to be transformed into the State. That is Rome and its dream. That is the third temptation of the devil. On the contrary, the State is transformed into the Church, will ascend and become a Church over the whole world – which is the complete opposite of Ultramontanism

---

43. Panichas, 'Dostoevsky and Roman Catholicism', p. 20.
44. Panichas, 'Dostoevsky and Roman Catholicism', p. 22.
45. Panichas, 'Dostoevsky and Roman Catholicism', pp. 23–24.
46. Panichas, 'Dostoevsky and Roman Catholicism', p. 25.

and Rome, and your interpretation, and is only the glorious destiny ordained for the Orthodox Church. This star will arise in the East!⁴⁷

Dostoevsky assumed that the outcome of Roman Catholicism was socialism and ultimately atheism.

Nicholas Berdyaev admits that Dostoevsky had a very superficial understanding of Catholicism and the story is directed more against the godless and materialistic philosophy of socialism, which is what the Grand Inquisitor holds. Socialism accepts the temptations Christ rejected, especially regarding changing stones into bread. The price for this miracle is the loss of freedom. Socialism has repudiated freedom for the sake of happiness of the masses. Worshipping this worldly kingdom, it has forfeited its spiritual freedom. Socialism is not so much a new religion as a reformed economic and social programme that promises people happiness in their short existence.⁴⁸

Further, atheistic socialism criticises Christianity for not guaranteeing happiness and giving adequate food to the people. Socialism promises bread and thus attracts millions of people. Christianity, however, does not violate the freedom of human beings but fulfils the words of Christ.⁴⁹ Throughout history, Christianity has been tempted to deny freedom to its believers. The yoke of freedom is a heavy burden, and it is a big struggle for Christianity to safeguard its integrity. Rejecting Christian liberty, the Church tends to favour the principle of authority.⁵⁰ But Berdyaev writes: 'Truth nailed upon the cross compels nobody, oppresses no one; it must be accepted and confessed freely; its appeal is addressed to free spirits.'⁵¹

Full of pity for human beings, the Grand Inquisitor is a socialist who conceals evil and presents it as something good. The teaching of the Antichrist is refined and appears to be benevolent. In fact, according to Berdyaev, there is a superficial resemblance between the 'evil antichristian principle and the good Christian principle' which poses a danger to the faithful. Berdyaev holds that 'the image of good begins to be "divided," Christ's image fades away and is merged into that of

---

47. Dostoevsky, *The Brothers Karamazov*, p. 57.
48. Nicholas Berdyaev, 'The Grand Inquisitor: Christ and Antichrist', in Dostoyevsky, *The Grand Inquisitor*, p. 74.
49. Berdyaev, 'The Grand Inquisitor: Christ and Antichrist', p. 71.
50. Berdyaev, 'The Grand Inquisitor: Christ and Antichrist', pp. 72–73.
51. Berdyaev, 'The Grand Inquisitor: Christ and Antichrist', p. 73.

Antichrist. Men appear with divided minds.'[52] The prose poem reveals Ivan's double-mindedness – his affinity with the Grand Inquisitor and his empathy with Christ.

Ivan's mind is a battlefield, tormented and divided. A 'split thinker,' he is, for example, willing to accept the existence of God but not the world he has created. Loving and loathing human beings at the same time, Ivan wonders what to do with humanity. The story of the Grand Inquisitor is his attempt to solve this dilemma – the renunciation of freedom for the sake of happiness. Some would think that though the Grand Inquisitor's argument is compelling, Christ's silence is more convincing. Ivan supports and scorns the ideology of the Grand Inquisitor. Dostoevsky now offers another solution in the Orthodox tradition – *sorbornost*.

## *Sorbornost*

The story of the Grand Inquisitor is about Christ versus organised religion. To solve this conflict, Dostoevsky advocates the concept of *sorbornost* (togetherness), a spiritual harmony based on unity in love, a free commitment to the tradition of catholicity as understood by the Orthodox Church. *Sorbornost* implies that 'we are all responsible for all'.[53] Father Zosima says,

> There is only one means of salvation … take yourself and make yourself responsible for all men's sins, that is the truth, you know, friends, for as soon as you sincerely make yourself responsible for everything and for all men, you will see at once that it is really so, and that you are to blame for everyone and for all things. But throwing your own indolence and impotence on others you will end by sharing the pride of Satan and murmuring against God.[54]

Responsibility means identifying and sharing the community's guilt as a fellow member. Dostoevsky claims that the Catholic Church has appropriated the freedom of its believers, while liberal Protestantism is too self-centred. Through Orthodoxy, Dostoevsky maintains a balance with this schema: Catholicism means 'unity without freedom', Protestantism 'freedom without unity'. The ideal church for him

---

52. Berdyaev, 'The Grand Inquisitor: Christ and Antichrist', pp. 74–75.
53. Dostoevsky, *The Brothers Karamazov*, p. 560.
54. Dostoevsky, *The Brothers Karamazov*, p. 299.

is Russian Orthodoxy, where there is 'freedom in unity and unity in freedom'.⁵⁵ He supports the idea of a state transformed into an ecclesiastical community, thus transferring the idea of *sobornost* into politics. This idea of a Russian theocracy is also defended, surprisingly, by Ivan.

In a published article about the ecclesiastical court, Ivan asserts 'that the Church ought to include the whole State, and not simply to occupy a corner in it, and, if this is, for some reason, impossible at present, then it ought, in reality, to be set up as the direct and chief aim of the future development of Christian society!'⁵⁶ Further, he adds, 'every earthly State should be, in the end, completely transformed into the Church and should become nothing else but a Church, rejecting every purpose incongruous with the aims of the Church'.⁵⁷ Except in Russia, this situation is unlikely to take place; the least the Church can hope for is some limited freedom. Through Ivan, the so-called atheist, Dostoevsky expresses his most cherished conviction regarding the Church – *sobornost*.

The Orthodox concept of *sobornost*, a spiritual harmony existing within a Christian community united in love and freedom, reminds us of the triune God. David S. Cunningham suggests that, from the trinitarian theological point of view, each of the three brothers does not need to represent a particular person in the Trinity. More importantly is the way the three relate to one another which underscores the trinitarian concept of *perichoresi*, the interpenetration of the three hypostases which unites them as one.⁵⁸

## Trinitarian Theology

The three legitimate brothers, Dmitri, Ivan and Alyosha, offer us an image of the Trinity. In fact, the number *three* is ever present in the novel – we have three lacerations, three confessions of the ardent heart, three temptations of Christ, parallelled by the three forces of the Grand Inquisitor, three meetings with Smerdyakov and three torments of the soul. The murder is related to Dmitri's need for 3,000 roubles. The *troika*,

---

55. Gibson, *The Religion of Dostoevsky*, p. 187.
56. Dostoevsky, *The Brothers Karamazov*, p. 52.
57. Dostoevsky, *The Brothers Karamazov*, p. 53.
58. David S. Cunningham, 'The Brothers Karamazov as Trinitarian Theology', in George Pattison and Diane Oenning Thompson (eds.), *Dostoevsky and the Christian Tradition* (Cambridge: Cambridge University Press, 2001), p. 144.

a Russian vehicle pulled by a team of three horses, is mentioned on three different occasions at Dmitri's trial. Fyodor was killed when he was hit three times by a paperweight weighing three pounds, and the murderer takes an envelope containing 3,000 roubles sealed with three wax seals.[59]

Further, each brother experiences some awakening: Alyosha while reading of the wedding at Cana, Dmitri at Mokroe and Ivan with the devil. Alyosha has to undergo three trials with Father Ferapont, Rakitin and Grushenka, while his brothers each have their own three trials as well. Father Zosima narrates his life with three interrelated events: Markel, the duel and the mysterious visitor. Dmitri has also to choose three options opened to him. Thus, the structure of *The Brothers Karamazov* is characterised by 'triplicity' demonstrating Dostoevsky's fascination for the 'tripartite' form. More than just a literary device, the number *three* has a spiritual and theological significance for him which may prompt us to read this novel as suggesting a trinitarian import.[60]

One can also interpret the three legitimate brothers as providing a structure for the story in accordance with St Augustine's understanding of the human psyche of 'being' 'knowing' and 'willing'. Driven by present passion, Dmitri simply 'is' (being), Ivan is the thinker (knowing) and Alyosha is 'willing' to leave the monastery to give witness to the Gospel in the world. The brothers can also be read as representing three aspects of human nature: mind (Ivan), body (Dmitri), spirit (Alyosha).[61]

The three voices in the novel express different ways of being a Karamazov, but they are all in one family. We can read it as the story of Dmitri, Ivan or Alyosha, but we must keep in mind that they are all members of the same family, good or bad. Cunningham writes: 'The three are truly "persons" in the most profound sense of the word, in that their individuality is defined by their relationships to others (they are, to a degree, "subsistent relations") But the three are also truly one; just as their given names divide them, so their family name draws them together.'[62] Thus, despite their failings, we must acknowledge that the family is created in the image of God and Christ is ever present in their lives: 'Hurrah for Karamazov.'[63]

---

59. Cunningham, 'The Brothers Karamazov as Trinitarian Theology', pp. 141–42.
60. Cunningham, 'The Brothers Karamazov as Trinitarian Theology', p. 142.
61. Cunningham, 'The Brothers Karamazov as Trinitarian Theology', p. 143.
62. Cunningham, 'The Brothers Karamazov as Trinitarian Theology', p. 145.
63. Dostoevsky, The Brothers Karamazov, p. 735.

## Chapter 7

## *The Power and the Glory*

## Graham Greene (1904-1991)

Graham Greene, one of the leading English novelists of the twentieth century, was born in Berkhamsted, Hertfordshire, England and died in Vevey, Switzerland. Greene attended Berkhamsted School where his father was the headmaster. After studying at Balliol College, Oxford, he converted to Roman Catholicism under the influence of Vivien Dayrell-Browning, whom he married in 1927. He worked as a copy-editor for *The Times* in London from 1926 to 1930. Greene's first novel was *The Man Within* (1929), later adapted as the movie, *The Smugglers* (1947). Leaving *The Times*, he worked as a film critic and editor for *The Spectator* till 1940. For the next three decades, he was a freelance journalist and writer, frequently travelling abroad.[1]

As the son of the headmaster, he was often bullied at school and because of this trauma, his writing is characterised by fear and anxiety:

> And so faith came to one – shapelessly, without dogma, a presence above a croquet lawn; something associated with violence, cruelty, evil across the way. One began to believe in heaven because one believed in hell, but for a long while, it

---

1. Amy Tikannen, 'Graham Greene', *Encyclopedia Britannica*, 13 May 2023, https://www.britannica.com/biography/Graham-Greene.

was only hell one could picture with a certain intimacy ... one began slowly, painfully, reluctantly to populate heaven.[2]

Harassed and depressed, Greene developed a suicidal tendency. His picture of hell is drawn from this harrowing existence, enhanced by literary inspiration.

Greene regarded himself as a Catholic who happened to write novels and not a Catholic writer as such. However, 'if Catholicism is not the very fabric of many of his texts, it is always a thread that helps to bind literary preoccupations into a recognizable pattern'.[3] Many of the characters in his novels are isolated Catholics who ponder the issue of damnation and redemption. Greene claimed that religious belief gives greater intensity and force to his characters than non-believers.[4] Consequently in his writings, he created his personal religious system in juxtaposition with the tenets of Catholicism.[5]

Thus, some critics accused Greene of heresies, such as Jansenism or Manichaeanism, because 'the space between the fallen nature of Greene's characters and the mysterious, inscrutable grace of God was too wide a theological gap to be countenanced, and Greene's disdain for traditional expressions of Catholic faith and piety portrayed throughout his novels proved troubling to many in the pre-Vatican II discourse of the Catholic Church'.[6] Detractors doubted the authenticity of Greene's Catholicism, given how he challenged Catholic orthodoxy. Be that as it may, fiction can sometimes surpass official Church teaching in conveying the reality of sin, forgiveness and redemption, and Greene's novels are exemplars.

The novels of Greene that are strongly influenced by his Catholic background include *Brighton Rock* (1938), *The Power and the Glory* (1940), *The Heart of the Matter* (1948) and *The End of the Affair* (1951). In these writings, Greene displays a consistent concern with sin and moral failure played out in squalid places that are dangerous and violent. His works on the moral and spiritual struggles of his protagonists set

---

2. Quoted in Bernard Bergonzi, *A Study in Greene: Graham Greene and the Art of the Novel* (Oxford: Oxford University Press, 2008), p. 105.
3. Mark Bosco, 'From *The Power and the Glory* to the *Honorary Consul*: The Development of Graham Greene's Catholic Imagination', *Religion and Literature* 36, no. 2 (2004), p. 51.
4. Bergonzi, *A Study in Greene*, 117.
5. Cates Baldridge, *Graham Greene's Fictions: The Virtues of Extremity* (Columbia, MO: University of Missouri Press, 2000), p. 4.
6. Bosco, 'From *The Power and the Glory* to the *Honorary Consul*, p. 52.

within a volatile political context enhances the conflict within the individuals. Inhabiting a fallen world, Greene's characters experience the presence of evil as an intense force. 'His deepest concerns were spiritual: a soul working out its salvation or damnation amid the paradoxes and anomalies of twentieth century existence.'[7]

Greene is a superb storyteller and his novels are thrillers featuring crimes and conspiracy, with thought-provoking dialogues incorporated within a fast-pace narrative. He greatly influenced many authors around the world, including Japanese writer Shusaku Endo. Known for his 1966 historical novel *Silence*, adapted into a film in 2016 by the director Martin Scorsese, Shusaku Endo is known as 'the Japanese Graham Greene'.[8] Like *The Power and the Glory*, *Silence* features a fugitive priest undergoing spiritual and moral struggles in the midst of fierce religious persecution, which is politically motivated. The Jesuit in *Silence*, too, falters in his priestly vocation as he confronts the terrifying prospect of martyrdom.

Focussing on *The Power and the Glory*, this chapter examines the difficulty of faith in the midst of persecution and poverty, the issues of sin and salvation, and the nature of priesthood shown through the figure of the 'bad' priest. Yet, in spite of the ruthless suppression of the Church and the priest's moral failure, his execution paradoxically represents the triumph of Christianity. Literary critic Terry Eagleton asserts that failure is 'one legitimate form of victory' in Greene's novels.[9] The priest seems to have 'a vested interest in failure', as we shall see in the following discussion.[10] Like a detective story set in Southern Mexico, with the police pursuing the priest, *The Power and the Glory* is full of surprises and suspense.

## Mexico

Graham Greene went to Mexico in the spring of 1930 to write a book on the condition of the Catholic Church in that country, where for several years it had been persecuted by an anti-religious government. Travelling in remote regions and experiencing physical hardship, he wrote his

---

7. From *The New York Times* obituary, 4 April 1991.
8. Christopher A. Link, 'Bad Priests and the Valor of Pity: Shusaku Endo and Graham Greene on the Paradoxes of Christian Virtue', *Logos* 15, no. 4 (2012), p. 75.
9. Bosco, 'From *The Power and the Glory* to the *Honorary Consul*, p. 57.
10. James Finn, 'Graham Greene as Moralist', *First Things* 3 (1990), p. 23.

masterpiece, *The Power and the Glory*. This novel, a powerful story based on his observations during a five-month trip to Tabasco in 1938, is 'vivid, conveying physical sensations with painful immediacy'.[11] In spite of the harsh conditions and suffering, Greene's visit to Mexico deepened his Catholic faith.

For Greene, there is a difference between faith and belief: 'faith ... means an unquestioning acceptance of God and a trust in His love and mercy. Belief, on the other hand, is man's rationalisation and institutionalisation of God through theology and the Church.'[12] Faith, a gift from God, is a spontaneous and instinctive response to the divine, while belief involves dogma and formula. 'Faith, one was told, could move mountains, and here was faith – faith in the spittle that healed the blind man and the voice that raised the dead.'[13] In the novel, belief associated with rituals seems mechanical and ceases to be vital to the faith. Greene also maintains that he is 'inclined to find superstition or magic more "rational" than such abstract religious ideas as the Holy Trinity'. He prefers the 'primitive manifestations of the faith',[14] as *The Power and the Glory* reveals.

In the 1930s, the revolutionary government in Mexico was hellbent on destroying Catholicism and declaring socialism and atheism as the guiding principles for the nation. This new policy meant that priests had to apostatise or face death. In the story, the government appears to be successful in its campaign to eradicate religion as we witness empty church buildings with no priests in sight. The only priest we encounter is the 'whisky priest', a morally weak cleric who has given in to the temptations of the flesh and is incompetent in performing his pastoral duties. Yet he chooses to remain in the socialist state – pursued relentlessly by the police lieutenant. The priest succeeds in evading the police for some time – when he is thrown in prison for a minor offence he is subsequently released. He also succeeds in crossing over to a more tolerant state but is compelled to return to hear the confession of a criminal, knowing full well that he will be arrested and executed eventually.

As the whisky priest faces death by the firing squad, he looks back at his life with painful disappointment. Unable to confess his sins to another priest, Padre Jose, who is too terrified to attend to him, the

---

11. Bergonzi, *A Study in Greene*, p. 103.
12. Quoted in Baldridge, *Graham Greene's Fictions*, p. 59.
13. Graham Greene, *The Power and the Glory* (New York: Penguin Classics, 2003), p. 155.
14. Quoted in Baldridge, *Graham Greene's Fictions*, p. 59.

priest thinks he will end up in hell. But Greene seems to say that our salvation does not depend on formula or ritual but on the mercy of God. Casting the figure of a guilt-ridden priest with allegorical or flat characters, Greene is able to present the story of sin and salvation, and corruption and contrition, in a dramatic and hypnotic way. While the priest is trying to evade being captured by the police, we can feel that the power of grace is also simultaneously pursuing him.

## Archetypal Characters

The journey of the priest can be perceived allegorically as the Way of the Cross, or in terms of Dantean circles, moving from Hell and Purgatory to Paradise. Whichever way we take it, the fundamental approach to measuring the priest's torturous path is 'to recognize that he carries his spiritual fidelity like a temptation among various contrasting characters'.[15] In other words, during the priest's pilgrimage, he meets different persons who reveal to him (and the reader) the various aspects of his character and the distance he has travelled towards his destination.

The priest first meets the dentist, Mr Tench, who feels forsaken and desires to escape from his oppressive environment. His name, Tench, sounds like a stench, which he has to endure as a dentist. In a festering land with buzzards flying around, Tench makes his living by treating people's tooth decay. As he spends his life looking into the depths of human decay, he, too, wants to escape. But unlike the priest, he is more interested in saving his peso than his soul. Both Tench and the priest have observed the boat leaving, but they remain in the wretched town for different reasons. For the priest, it is his pastoral duty; for Tench, it is his personal monetary considerations.

Coral Fellows, a 13-year-old girl, tells the priest that she lost her faith at age 10. Very mature for her age, she takes good care of her mother and those who need her: 'She was ready to accept any responsibility, even that of vengeance, without a second thought. It was her life.'[16] It is a significant encounter as Coral provides the priest with food, drink and refuge and helps him to escape. Even though she has lost her Protestant faith, she is compassionate and sympathetic towards the plight of the priest. Coral said, 'I hope you'll escape … If they kill you I shan't forgive them – ever.'[17]

---

15. Georg Gaston, *The Pursuit of Salvation: A Critical Guide to the Novels of Graham Greene* (Troy, NY: Whitston Pub. Co., 1984), p. 30.
16. Greene, *The Power and the Glory*, p. 42.
17. Greene, *The Power and the Glory*, p. 42.

The priest returns to the village where he had fathered a child with Maria. Seeing his daughter Brigida for the first time in years, he feels as if he was 'seeing his own mortal sin look back at him, without contrition'.[18] The priest is concerned that his child will face corruption when she discovers that 'the world was in her heart already, like the small spot of decay in a fruit'. 'She was without protection – she had no grace, no charm to plead for her; his heart was shaken by the conviction of loss.' The priest thus offers a silent prayer thinking only of her welfare: 'O God, give me any kind of death – without contrition, in a state of sin – only save this child.'[19] Through this act of unconditional and sacrificial love, we discover God's true nature: 'one must love every soul as if it were one's own child'. The priest also feels a 'tethered and aching' love for his child.[20] Unable to provide his child with a secure home, he trusts to God's mercy.

Upon meeting the half-caste, who turns out to be Judas, the traitor, instead of reacting with anger and self-pity, the priest realises his tendency for such treacherous deeds. He attempts to understand and accept his betrayer: 'Christ had died for this man too: how could he pretend with his pride and lust and cowardice to be any more worthy of that death than this half-caste?'[21] Looking at his betrayer, the priest experiences a vision of divine love, which helps him to show charity to every sinner he encounters.

The priest's pilgrimage is also a 'process of purgation'.[22] During one night in a prison cell, he finds himself in the presence of many other offenders, which reveals his past sins and the sins of humanity in general. Nevertheless, these inmates are related to him as fellow sinners who should be accepted and loved. The priest's sympathy is shown when he empathises and defends a couple making love in the dark corner of the cell, while a respectable middle-class woman, who is jailed for possessing religious books in her home, is scandalised. 'Because suddenly we discover that our sins have so much beauty' and 'Hate was just a failure of imagination'.[23]

The prison presents the reality of life to the priest: 'this place was very like the world: overcrowded with lust and crime and unhappy love:

---

18. Greene, *The Power and the Glory*, p. 67.
19. Greene, *The Power and the Glory*, p. 82.
20. Greene, *The Power and the Glory*, p. 82.
21. Greene, *The Power and the Glory*, p. 99.
22. Gaston, *The Pursuit of Salvation*, p. 31.
23. Greene, *The Power and the Glory*, pp. 130–31.

it stank to heaven; but he realized that after all it was possible to find peace there, when you knew for certain that the time was short'.[24] The experience in prison has a significant effect on him as he experiences a profound sense of solidarity with sinners: 'He was just one criminal among a herd of criminals … he had a sense of companionship which he had never received in the old days when pious people came kissing his black cotton glove.'[25] Although the people in prison have committed sins of lust, anger, pride, etc., the priest is able to discover beauty, as he tells the pious lady who is upset by the couple having sex:

> Such a lot of beauty. Saints talk about the beauty of suffering. Well, we are not saints, you and I. Suffering to us is just ugly. Stench and crowding and pain. That is beautiful in that corner – to them. It needs a lot of learning to see things with a saint's eye: a saint gets a subtle taste for beauty and can look down on poor ignorant palates like theirs. But we can't afford to.[26]

Here we witness the priest possessing the feeling of holiness and humility. His humility moves him to escape the police and flee to another state. Seeing himself as a sinner, he feels that staying put would be an insult to God and the Church that he represents. Crossing the border, he finds a place of refuge with the Lehr family: 'Mr. Lehr had left Germany when he was a boy to escape military service: he had a shrewd lined idealistic face. You needed to be shrewd in this country if you were going to retain any ideals at all: he was cunning in the defence of the good life.'[27] But the priest is not satisfied with this kind of comfortable life and remembers the night in the crowded cell filled with fellow sinners.

Once the priest enters into the safe territory where the Lehr family lives, free from physical harm, as he recalls the past, he becomes aware of the spiritual danger that comes with a comfortable lifestyle: 'He felt respect all the way up the street: men took off their hats as he passed: it was as if he had got back to the days before the persecution. He could feel the old life hardening round him like a habit, a stony case which held his head high and dictated the way he walked, and even formed his

---

24. Greene, *The Power and the Glory*, p. 125.
25. Greene, *The Power and the Glory*, p. 128.
26. Greene, *The Power and the Glory*, p. 130.
27. Greene, *The Power and the Glory*, p. 161.

words.'[28] Ironically, the priest feels relief when the half-caste appears to lure him back across the border, where he would be arrested.

In his writings, Greene often explores geographical frontiers with peace and safety on one side and danger and death on the other. There are also non-physical boundaries that he examines, such as the difference between Catholicism and Communism, success and failure, faith and doubt, trust and betrayal. In this case, Greene considers the 'temptation' that lures the priest back to the dangerous spot. This consideration reveals his 'sympathy with the seedy, the outcast, the apparently disloyal, a sympathy that has at times come close to collusion. He seems, indeed, to have a vested interest in failure.'[29]

The appearance of the half-caste seems like a temptation he cannot resist – 'the temptation of self-sacrifice'.[30] The return of the Judas figure to tempt him back is a clear sign that God, not the lieutenant, is the real hunter. Aware that it is a trap, the priest actually

> felt quite cheerful: he had never really believed in this peace. He had dreamed of it so often on the other side that now it meant no more to him than a dream. He began to whistle a tune – something he had heard somewhere once. 'I found a rose in my field': it was time he woke up.[31]

Thus the priest returns to minister to the needy, convinced that it is God's will.

As a cleric without a name, he represents the vocation of the priesthood, which he fulfils as best as he can despite his defects and moral failings. According to the Letter to the Hebrews, 'For we do not have a high priest who is unable to sympathize with our weaknesses, but we have one who in every respect has been tested as we are, yet without sin' (14:5). The only perfect person is Christ, the high priest who understands our frailty. The whisky priest is not the Lord, but a sinful human being struggling to fulfil his vocation while facing difficulties and temptations. The bishop and almost all the other priests have fled to safety. Only he remains. This priest is contrasted with Padre Jose, who, following the government's demands, has abandoned the priesthood

---

28. Greene, *The Power and the Glory*, pp. 167–68.
29. Finn, 'Graham Greene as Moralist', p. 23.
30. Gaston, *The Pursuit of Salvation*, p. 33.
31. Greene, *The Power and the Glory*, p. 180.

and married. Padre Jose is even afraid to hear the confession of the priest waiting to be executed.

The death of this 'bad priest' is contrasted with Juan, a saintly priest that appears in a pious book that a mother reads to her son. The boy is also the one who welcomes a new priest into the country. This signifies to us that the mission of the Church continues. Tertullian, a second-century Church Father says: 'The blood of the martyrs is the seed of the church.' The mission of the Church continues in Mexico today due to the examples of martyrdom, the glorious one like that of Juan and the 'inglorious death' of the nameless priest.[32] They are all instrumental to the spread of the Christian faith amid fierce persecution by a godless and totalitarian government.

## Martyrdom

'The Mexicans are not only the people who killed the martyrs; they are the people for whom the martyrs died.'[33] *The Power and the Glory* is also about the journey of a modern martyr, a nameless Mexican priest, who acknowledges his sinfulness, but continues to minister to his people in disguise, celebrating masses and hearing confessions. He embarks on this mission of mercy, knowing well that he will be arrested and killed. Eventually, like Christ, he was betrayed, interrogated and executed.

A flawed cleric, who has been denied absolution before he is executed, Greene attempts to portray him as a martyr. Drunk and desperate, when taken to his execution, 'you could tell that he was doing his best – it was only that his legs were not fully under his control'.[34] The whisky priest could be considered a martyr because he responds to the call of duty as a priest at the cost of his own life. Greene considers him a saint as well:

> He felt only an immense disappointment because he had to go to God empty-handed, with nothing done at all. It seemed to him at that moment that it would have been quite easy to have been a saint. It would only have needed a little self-restraint and a little courage. He felt like someone who has missed

---

32. Gordon Leah, 'A Bad Priest? Reflections on Regeneration in Graham Green's Novel *The Power and the Glory*', *Heythrop Journal* 51, no. 1 (2010), p. 21.
33. Quoted in Bergonzi, *A Study in Greene*, p. 110.
34. Greene, *The Power and the Glory*, p. 216.

happiness by seconds at an appointed place. He knew now that at the end there was only one thing that counted – to be a saint.[35]

Greene upholds the Church's teaching that a man should be distinguished from his office. *The Power and the Glory* examines the nature of the Catholic priesthood and the sacraments. The priest character in the novel is 'ontological in nature', set apart not by his virtue but by his sacramental function.[36] When Coral asks the priest to renounce his priesthood to save himself, he replies, 'It's impossible. There's no way. I'm a priest. It's out of my power.'[37]

*Ex opere operato* is a Latin expression which means 'by the work worked'. The sacraments confer grace when the sign is validly effected. The sacraments take effect as long as the priest celebrates the mass, hears confessions, etc., using the proper form and formula. Its validity does not depend on the character of the priest administering it. The priest in the novel admits his unworthiness – he is a 'whisky priest', fond of drinking and has fathered a child. However, instead of fleeing to other states where he would be safe, or abandoning the priesthood to remain alive, he persists in bringing the sacraments to his flock in spite of the danger.

Further, the priest is contrite and humble, and never fails to mortify himself when his conscience comes into play. He tells the lieutenant he is proud to be the only priest remaining in the province when others have fled. He disagrees when the lieutenant says he will be a martyr: 'Oh, no. Martyrs are not like me. They don't think all the time – if I had drunk more brandy I shouldn't be so afraid.'[38]

*The Power and the Glory* exposes the 'paradoxes of sainthood' when we witness a fallen priest who goes against the instinct of self-preservation and dies for his faith.[39] God makes use of the weak to accomplish his work. St Paul says, 'For the sake of Christ, then, I am content with weaknesses, insults, hardships, persecutions, and calamities; for when I am weak, then I am strong' (2 Cor. 12:10). Thus the lieutenant and the half-caste who are responsible for the priest's death are also part of

---

35. Greene, *The Power and the Glory*, p. 210.
36. Bosco, 'From *The Power and the Glory* to the *Honorary Consul*, p. 63.
37. Greene, *The Power and the Glory*, p. 40.
38. Greene, *The Power and the Glory*, p. 196.
39. David Pryce-Jones, *Graham Greene* (Edinburgh: Oliver, 1963), p. 57.

God's purpose. In other words, they are part of divine providence – God is present in all human actions. Greene writes:

> But at the centre of his own faith there always stood the convincing mystery – that we were made in God's image – God was the parent, but He was also the policeman, the criminal, the priest, the maniac, and the judge. Something resembling God dangled from the gibbet or went into odd attitudes before the bullets in a prison yard or contorted itself like a camel in the attitude of sex. He would sit in the confessional and hear the complicated dirty ingenuities which God's image had thought out: and God's image shook now, up and down on the mule's back, with the yellow teeth sticking out over the lower lip; and God's image did its despairing act of rebellion with Maria in the hut among the rats.[40]

Since all human actions are images of God, the responsibility of the character is limited. They all share in this 'inescapable existence conditioned by their Maker'.[41] Thus, individuals cannot be judged or distinguished solely by their actions. If we believe in God, *The Power and the Glory* is not just a thriller about a policeman chasing after a priest in Mexico but a divine comedy addressing our fall and redemption.

Infused with Christian imagery, the main characters have no names – they are allegorical figures. Contrasting the idealism of the lieutenant to the fatalism of the priest, both characters stand by their beliefs to the end. The lieutenant sincerely believes that he kills to protect the people while the whisky priest continues to give life in his mission. The allegory emerges to reinforce the Christian story: the priest who has been betrayed, suffered and died for his sins has saved and converted others by his good examples. The lieutenant, like Pilate, falls asleep due to exhaustion: 'He couldn't remember afterwards anything of his dreams except laughter.'[42] The American criminal, Calver, sounds like Calvary, and the two photographs at the police station remind us of Christ and Barabbas.

---

40. Greene, *The Power and the Glory*, p. 101.
41. Pryce-Jones, *Graham Greene*, p. 58.
42. Greene, *The Power and the Glory*, p. 207.

## Dostoevskian Echoes

In *The Power and the Glory*, which appears to show the triumph of Christianity over secularism, we hear echoes of the Russian novelist Dostoevsky resounding in some of Greene's characters. For example, the discussion between the priest and the police lieutenant regarding ultimate values in Greene's novel reminds us of the conversation between Christ and the Grand Inquisitor in *The Brothers Karamazov*. The incompatibility of their beliefs is well depicted in this exchange:

> We've always said the poor are blessed and the rich are going to find it hard to get into heaven. Why should we make it hard for the poor man too? Oh, I know we are told to give to the poor, to see they are not hungry – hunger can make a man do evil just as much as money can. But why should we give the poor power? It's better to let him die in dirt and wake in heaven – so long as we don't push his face in the dirt.'
>
> 'I hate your reasons,' the lieutenant said. 'I don't want reasons. If you see somebody in pain, people like you reason and reason. You say – perhaps pain's a good thing, perhaps he'll be better for it one day. I want to let my heart speak.'
>
> 'At the end of a gun.'
>
> 'Yes. At the end of a gun.'
>
> 'Oh, well, perhaps when you're my age you'll know the heart's an untrustworthy beast. The mind is too, but it doesn't talk about love. Love. And a girl puts her head under water or a child's strangled, and the heart all the time says love, love.'[43]

Like the priest's secular counterpart, the lieutenant 'was a mystic, too, and what he had experienced was vacancy – a complete certainty in the existence of a dying, cooling world, of human beings who had evolved from animals for no purpose at all'.[44]

As in Dostoevsky's novel, Greene uses 'mirroring and doubling' as a structural device.[45] The priest and the lieutenant stand in opposition to each other by their beliefs, social and political circumstances. It is the duty and responsibility of the lieutenant to arrest who he believes to be

---

43. Greene, *The Power and the Glory*, p. 199.
44. Greene, *The Power and the Glory*, pp. 24–25.
45. Kenneth C. Pellow, 'The "Presence" of Dostoevsky in Graham Greene's *The Power and the Glory*', *Renascence* 67, no. 1 (2015), p. 59.

the last active priest in the region. He says, 'We do more good when we catch one of these [priests]' than catching the American bank robber and murderer.[46] Unlike the hedonistic priest, the lieutenant is an ascetic: 'he felt no need of women' and the room he lives is 'as comfortless as a prison or a monastic cell'.[47] In fact, he 'felt no sympathy at all with the weakness of the flesh'.[48]

The lieutenant still remembers 'the smell of incense in the churches of his boyhood, the candles and the laciness and the self-esteem, the immense demands made from the altar steps by men who didn't know the meaning of sacrifice'.[49] Regarding his attitude towards religious belief, which is practical and rational, the lieutenant resembles the Grand Inquisitor.

The priest is concerned with saving the souls of his flock, even though he endangers some in the process. On the other hand, the lieutenant is determined to improve his people's lives, especially the children: 'It infuriated him to think that there were still people in the state who believed in a loving and merciful God.'[50] He believes the children 'deserved nothing less than the truth – a vacant universe and a cooling world, the right to be happy in any way they chose'.[51] His method is similar to the Grand Inquisitor in that he would provide 'bread' for the people and secure their obedience by means of fear, not freedom.

With good intentions, the lieutenant is determined to eradicate what he perceives as the evil of the Church and her teaching: 'No more money for saying prayers, no more money for building places to say prayers in. We'll give people food instead, teach them to read, give them books. We'll see they don't suffer.'[52] But the priest believes suffering is part and parcel of life, whether in the secular or sacred sphere:

> It's no good your working for your end unless you're a good man yourself. And there won't always be good men in your party. Then you'll have all the old starvation, beating, get-rich-anyhow. But it doesn't matter so much my being a coward – and all the rest. I can put God into a man's mouth

---

46. Greene, *The Power and the Glory*, p. 23.
47. Greene, *The Power and the Glory*, pp. 23–24.
48. Greene, *The Power and the Glory*, p. 25.
49. Greene, *The Power and the Glory*, p. 22.
50. Greene, *The Power and the Glory*, p. 24.
51. Greene, *The Power and the Glory*, p. 58.
52. Greene, *The Power and the Glory*, p. 94.

just the same – and I can give him God's pardon. It wouldn't make any difference to that if every priest in the Church was like me.[53]

Here again, Greene distinguishes the man and the sacrament he administers, putting 'God into man's mouth' and giving him 'God's pardon'. It does not matter if the priest is bad, the sacraments he confers are valid all the same.

The lieutenant admires the priest's conviction and fidelity but sees no meaning in it. Like the priest, he has dedicated his life to justice. As they journey back to the city for trial and execution, the lieutenant tells the priest that even his God is not grateful for his service and has rewarded his loyalty with cruelty. Then accepting his fate and believing in the mystery of God's grace, the priest says, 'I don't know a thing about the mercy of God: I don't know how awful the human heart looks to Him. But I do know this – that if there's ever been a single man in this state damned, then I'll be damned too … I wouldn't want it to be any different. I just want justice, that's all.'[54] Despite human failure and uncontrolled passion, the priest 'knew now that at the end there was only one thing that counted – to be a saint'.[55]

As a channel of grace, the priest's presence has a benign influence on those around him, a spiritual power that energises souls. He brings 'back to … secular and desiccated consciousness an impression of spiritual greatness and possibility, indirectly moving them, perhaps at an unconscious level, to a greater spiritual moment in themselves'.[56] For example, after a chance encounter with the priest, Mr Tench the dentist decides to contact his wife, whom he has not seen for years: 'an odd impulse had come to him to project this stray letter towards the last address he had … He tried to begin … He began to write …'[57] Coral Fellows, who harbours the outlaw priest, is given an opportunity to discuss religion. This moves her to reflect on her faith which she had abandoned at the age of ten.[58]

---

53. Greene, *The Power and the Glory*, p. 195.
54. Greene, *The Power and the Glory*, p. 200.
55. Greene, *The Power and the Glory*, p. 210.
56. Quoted in Baldridge, *Graham Greene's Fictions*, p. 61.
57. Greene, *The Power and the Glory*, pp. 45–46.
58. Greene, *The Power and the Glory*, p. 41.

## Paradox

In the novel, the priest serves as the embodiment of belief, and the police lieutenant of unbelief. A paradoxical figure, the priest possesses a 'double rhythm of hope and despair, action and passivity, vaunting ambition and victimization, longing for escape and for capture, obsession equally with the diurnal and the transcendent moment'.[59] A morally weak individual who is addicted to alcohol and has fathered a child, the priest is mediocre at best.

On the other hand, the lieutenant, the priest's counterpart, is a puritanical law enforcer who dedicated his life to his socialist ideals. Being a celibate and performing his police duties with religious zeal, he would have been an ideal candidate for the priesthood: 'There was something of a priest in his intent observant walk – a theologian going back over the errors of the past to destroy them again.'[60] Indeed, Greene stresses the lieutenant's asceticism, dedication and honesty.

The lieutenant's anti-clericalism stems from his conviction that the Church is solely responsible for the injustice in the country. He perceives the priesthood as a corrupt system that benefits only a few. To arrest a priest, the lieutenant would go to the extent of shooting hostages. At the same time, he offers to bring Padre Jose to hear the confession of the whisky priest before his execution.

Like the French existentialists such as Albert Camus and Jean-Paul Sartre, Greene struggles with a world that seems meaningless – a dystopia, as it were. However, his Catholic faith gives him hope and, in some ways, offsets 'the vacancy and aridity he so powerfully describes'.[61] Without this faith and doubt, his writings lack passion and purpose. Yet, aware of the difficulties of faith, Greene also experiences the desperation of disbelief. Greene thinks that humanity's 'predicament is paradoxical'.[62] In other words, the person's goodness and greatness are intermingled with his greatness and wretchedness.

An Augustinian, Greene seems to hold that the fall of man is not just the loss of faith, hope and charity but a corruption that leads to lust and pride. At the same time, the human person, too, feels a sense of responsibility and shame and seeks to save himself. Pascal

---

59. Quoted in Nettie Cloete, 'Religious Paradoxes in Graham Greene's Novels', *Koers* 63, no. 4 (1998), p. 318.
60. Greene, *The Power and the Glory*, p. 24.
61. Quoted in Clyde Penrose St Amant, 'God Gets his Man: A Study of Graham Greene', *Perspectives in Religious Studies* 1, no. 1 (1974), p. 56.
62. St Amant, 'God Gets his Man', p. 57.

maintains that 'Christianity is strange. It bids man recognize that he is vile, even abominable, and bids him desire to be like God. Without such a counterpoise, this dignity would make him horribly vain, or this humiliation would make him terribly abject.'[63] This paradox is portrayed in *The Power and the Glory* when the priest reflects on the anomaly of his clerical state. 'Looked at rationally, the priest is all too often a mess – but it is here, in spite of all, that we see the power and the glory in a world of saints and sinners.'[64]

For Greene, the person is simultaneously good and evil, an ambiguity that is powerfully played out in his novel. His characters are not mere mechanical entities; they experience the conflict between good and evil and thus have to make their choice. In *The Power and the Glory*, the priest, deeply aware of his sinfulness, attempts to flee from God: 'Evil ran like malaria in his veins.'[65] However, he tells himself that 'In three days … I shall have confessed and been absolved.'[66] The priest admits that he has more pride than the love of God.[67] But Paul says, 'where sin increased, grace abounded all the more' (Rom. 5:21). Thus, in the end, 'the bad priest' realises that to be a saint is what really matters.

## The 'Bad Priest'

> There are good priests and bad priests. It is just that I am a bad priest.[68]

The figure of the bad priest is not just an archetype but a terrifying reality as we have witnessed the spate of clerical abuses and misconduct throughout history. He is a character clearly 'fraught with background'.[69] Bad priests have been part of the fabric of religious life. In the Old Testament, the bad priest appears almost immediately after the institution of the priesthood. Apostasy occurred when Aaron, the chief priest, yielded to the demands of the Israelites to build the golden calf (Exod. 32). Aaron, the traditional founder and head of the Israelite

---

63. Quoted in St Amant, 'God Gets his Man', pp. 57–58.
64. David Jasper, 'The Priest in the Novels of Graham Greene', *Theology* 124, no. 2 (2021), p. 84.
65. Greene, *The Power and the Glory*, p. 176.
66. Greene, *The Power and the Glory*, p. 176.
67. Greene, *The Power and the Glory*, p. 196.
68. Greene, *The Power and the Glory*, p. 191.
69. Quoted in Link, 'Bad Priests', p. 79.

priesthood, became the first person to break the Covenant, breaking the command, 'You shall not make for yourself an idol, whether in the form of anything that is in heaven above, or that is on the earth beneath, or that is in the water under the earth' (Exod. 20:4). In the New Testament, the Pharisees and the Sadducees, the high priests, Annas and Caiaphas, are examples of bad priests in the biblical tradition.

In Western literature, such as the writings of Boccaccio and Chaucer, we find the figure of the bad priest portrayed as a buffoon, the 'reverent rake'.[70] Historical figures like Tomás de Torquemada of the Spanish Inquisition and the Grand Inquisitor in *The Brothers Karamazov* are well known for their zeal in torturing and burning heretics. Unfortunately, the reality of the bad priest in the Catholic Church has been constantly in the media in the last few decades to the extent that the good priest is sometimes perceived as the exception rather than the norm. This widespread abuse and misconduct by bad priests has grievously hurt the Church's credibility, leading to a crisis of faith among many believers.

In *The Power and the Glory*, however, the portrayal of the bad priest is meant to be 'a theological test case of the limits of divine mercy'.[71] He bears the 'emblematic weight of sin, brought … fully to consciousness in the commission'.[72] The bad priest in Greene's novel is an example of German theologian Karl Rahner's 'man as a being threatened radically by guilt'.[73] The presence of the bad priest serves the purpose of leading the reader to reflect on the question of redemption and damnation.

The portrayal of the bad priest is Greene's attempt to present the Christian paradox (Rom. 5:6-10) and theodicy, justifying God in the face of evil. This theodicy is reflected in the sermon given by the priest to a group of peasants:

> Pray that you will suffer more and more and more. Never get tired of suffering. The police watching you, the soldiers gathering taxes, the beating you always get from the jefe because you are too poor to pay, smallpox and fever, hunger … that is all part of heaven – the preparation. Perhaps without them – who can tell? – you wouldn't enjoy heaven so much. Heaven would not be complete.[74]

---

70. Link, 'Bad Priests', p. 80.
71. Link, 'Bad Priests', p. 80.
72. Link, 'Bad Priests', p. 81.
73. Quoted in Link, 'Bad Priests', p. 81.
74. Greene, *The Power and the Glory*, p. 69.

The priest believing himself to be bad, cut off from grace, unaware of his virtue, is, in reality, a compassionate person, willing to sacrifice his life for others. He is an example of what Christ teaches, 'do not let your left hand know what your right hand is doing' (Matt. 6:3).

## The Catholic Novel

Muriel Spark, a Catholic novelist, said there is no such thing as a 'Catholic Novel'. George Orwell thought Catholics were unlikely to be good writers because their religious tradition or 'the atmosphere of orthodoxy' might hinder their creativity. Orwell claimed that the novel is, in fact, a Protestant literary form, the product of a free and independent mind.[75] But the tension created by orthodoxy and free thinking can be creative, imaginative and inspiring in prose writing, as Graham Greene has shown us in his novel.

In its effort to control literary work, the Catholic Church almost banned *The Power and the Glory*. The Vatican was trying to prevent heresy which had spread into the academic world. The Holy Office considered the book dangerous and advised the author to correct certain defects, which Greene politely refused to do. Cardinal Griffin of Westminster asked him not to allow reprints of translations of *The Power and the Glory* without making appropriate corrections. Rome complained that the book emphasised man's 'wretchedness' and 'portrayed a state of affairs so paradoxical and erroneous that it would disconcert an unenlightened person'.[76]

Further, the Holy Office complained that the book displayed an 'abnormal propensity towards situations in which one kind of sexual immorality or another plays a role'. Vatican officials suggested that Greene should be informed that 'literature of this kind does harm to the cause of the true religion' and that 'in the future he should behave more cautiously'.[77] They insisted that the novel 'posed a danger to the virtue of the majority' because of its 'odd and paradoxical' views. Greene replied that 'the aim of the book was to oppose the power of the sacraments and the indestructibility of the church on the one hand with, on the

---

75. Bergonzi, *A Study in Greene*, p. 137.
76. 'How Rome Tried to Censor Greene's Masterpiece', *The Guardian*, https://www.theguardian.com/uk/2001/jul/08/books.humanities.
77. 'How Rome Tried to Censor'.

other, the merely temporal power of an essentially Communist state.'[78] In fact, the novel highlights the resilience of the Church in the face of persecution.

Cardinal Montini, then in the Vatican Secretariat of State, who was to become Pope Paul VI in 1963, took a more balanced view of Greene's book. He said, 'I have no objection to make to the just observations in the [censure of] this work. But it seems to me that, in such a judgment, there is lacking a sense of the work's substantial merits.' He also pointed to the 'heroic fidelity to his own ministry within the innermost soul of a priest who is in many respects reprehensible'. Thus, while the Holy Office was critical of the novel, Pope Paul VI, who had read the book himself, told Greene, 'Some aspects of your books are certain to offend some Catholics, but you should pay no attention to that.'[79]

*The Power and the Glory* has been regarded as Greene's finest work. Perhaps some aspects of the book might be offensive to some pious Catholics, as Paul VI had pointed out. It might be the intention of the author to jolt believers out of their complacency and comfort zone. However, in Greene's story, we follow the journey of a sinner and saint, the story of sin and salvation, feeling the struggle, doubt and final resolution. The whisky priest's path of sainthood is marked by fear, temptation and betrayal as he attempts to escape persecution by the state. The appearance of another priest at the end signifies resurrection and the triumph of Christianity – for thine is the Kingdom, the Power and the Glory. This novel reflects Greene's understanding of human existence as essentially infernal and that the only way to peace and happiness is to follow the vision of God.

---

78. Quoted in Heather Moreland McHale, 'Graham Greene's Pope: Finding God in Battered Places', *America* 213, no. 15 (2015), p. 22.
79. Quoted in McHale, 'Graham Greene's Pope', p. 22.

# Conclusion

Has the Church made up its mind on literature with thought-provoking themes? How will the relationship between Christianity and Western literature evolve? Overall, is literature doing justice to the gospel vision?

First we discussed Augustine's thoughts on creation and sin in *Confessions*. Influenced by Neoplatonism and the Pauline letters, *Confessions* grew out of Augustine's criticism of Manichaeism. Most of his writings were written against the backdrop of this dualistic philosophy and its influence can still be traced in some of his works. It was Augustine's reading of Neoplatonism supported by the Scriptures under the guidance of Ambrose of Milan that paved the way for his reception into the Catholic Church. *Confessions* is about Augustine returning to the faith of his childhood. It was a conversion from a life of rakishness to a life of righteousness.

Since the *Confessions* was written after his conversion, Augustine tends to be oversensitive and exaggerate his shortcomings and moral failure. Thus he accuses himself of sinning when, as an adolescent, he chooses playing over studying. He also maintains that he has sinned in preferring secular literature such as Virgil's *Aeneid* to writing and arithmetic. Augustine believes he is wrong to have spent his time on pagan classics instead of studying the Scriptures, preferring Virgil to Moses, as it were. But it is Cicero's *Hortensius*, a philosophical work, that inspires him to pursue truth. Cicero prompts him to read the Bible, although he complains that the style is too simplistic. Further, it is through 'certain books of the Platonist' that Augustine begins to think of God and the soul in spiritual terms. Thus, in spite of his criticism of pagan literature, it is the classics that compel Augustine to discover the truth in the Scriptures.

Focussing on *Inferno* (Hell) and *Purgatorio* (Purgatory) in the *Divine Comedy*, we have discussed Dante's portrayal of sin and its punishment. Dante's reflection on sin is aided by his reading of Augustine, Aquinas and Averroes. In this epic poem, Virgil is Dante's guide through Hell

# Conclusion

and Purgatory. Virgil was chosen by Dante because he was the greatest of the Roman poets. Influenced by Virgil, the theme of love runs through Dante's work. As a poet who emphasises love, Virgil was perhaps the most Christian of all the classical authors. In the *Divine Comedy*, the first time we encounter Virgil is when Dante is unable to ascend the mountain, being blocked by three ferocious creatures. Accompanied by Virgil, Dante is able to overcome the obstacles in his ascent to Mount Purgatory and then to Paradise with the help of Beatrice.

Starting as pilgrim and guide, the bond between Dante and Virgil develops into one of father and son as they reach Purgatory. Like most relationships between father and son, there are moments of conflict and estrangement as they learn to trust one another. Their self-giving love stands in dialectical contrast to what Hell is like: betrayal, denial of truth and lovelessness. The love and friendship fostered by Dante and Virgil enable them to persevere through Hell. As Virgil writes in the *Eclogues*, a collection of short poems, *omnia vincit amor* (love conquers all).

As a Renaissance writer, Shakespeare was steeped in the classics. His early education in grammar school exposed him to Roman literature, history and rhetoric. When he moved to London to work as a playwright, he read deeply in Ovid, Virgil, Cicero, Horace and Seneca. It was this grounding in the classics that gave Shakespeare's plays such a universal appeal. As Ben Jonson says, he was 'not for an age but for all time'. This classical tradition enhanced the depth and force of his imagination.

In his plays, Shakespeare moves beyond creed and dogma, conveying the Christian vision through dramatic representation. He brought the Bible to the playhouse, as it were. As we have seen, *Hamlet* and *The Tempest* are imbued with biblical imagery and Christian symbolism.

Despite his strong disapproval of myths and the rest of pagan writings in *Paradise Regained*, Milton continues to use stories of gods and goddesses when he judges them appropriate to support his genre and theme. Acutely aware of their poetic value, he uses these fables with great originality, subordinating mythic imagery to his overall Christian vision. Pagan mythology is incorporated in Milton's poems, not for doctrinal purposes but to enhance his literary style. Known for their powerful visual effect, classical myths and metaphors function as a structural device for Milton's imagery in *Paradise Lost*. His use of them is 'proleptic' in that each image contributes to the anticipation of key events of the poem and gives us a sense of what is going to happen.[1]

---

1. Jonathan Howard Collett, 'Milton's Use of Classical Mythology in "Paradise Lost"', *PMLA : Publications of the Modern Language Association of America* 85, no. 1 (1970), p. 88.

Milton manipulates classical myths in three significant ways in *Paradise Lost*. First, in the tradition which regards devils as heathen gods, such as Satan and his crew; second, in the description of Eden and its inhabitants in graphic imagery; third, in the introduction of myths similar to those revealed in the Old and New Testament in Book XI that Adam will receive.[2] Milton's achievement in *Paradise Lost* lies in his use of the English language's rhythm, sound and structure. It is a distinctively Christian poem that is classically inspired.

The Romantic movement of the late eighteenth and mid-nineteenth century was characterised by concern for the individual and his transcendental aspirations. The emphasis is on the subjective and spiritual aspects of the person. Romanticism led to a deepened awareness of the beauty of nature, the exaltation of emotion over reason and the senses over intellect. The focus is on the human person, temperament and mental faculties. In literature, understood more as a genre than a philosophy, Romanticism is concerned with the genius, the hero or exceptional individual, with his passion and inner struggles. Against strict adherence to formal rules and tradition, the artist is seen as a creator, emphasising the imagination as a guide to transcendental experience and truth. Romanticism, in its preoccupation with the mystical, subconscious and supernatural, is also a movement against the Enlightenment, technological encroachment and extreme rationalism.

While upholding the basic beliefs of Christianity, Romanticism profoundly influenced how Christian ideas were discussed and taught. Concerned more with faith than doctrine, it promoted a sacramental vision of life where there is a sense of God's incarnate presence in all things, especially in nature, which reveals the sacredness of the world. Every creature and created thing can be a revelation of divine presence. Having a sacramental vision of life means that we grow in greater awareness of our kinship with the whole created order, as revealed in Coleridge's *The Rime of the Ancient Mariner*.

While Romanticism flourished in England and France, the realist novel emerged in Russia. The nineteenth century is considered the Golden Age for Russian literature. It was a significant period for the novel, with extremely long stories featuring in-depth descriptions of individuals with tortured personalities. Weaving the historical context with his characters and the conflict that consumed them, Dostoevsky was the master of such epic narratives. Though he wrote within the Russian context, he is considered a universal writer. Breaking with

---

2. Collett, 'Milton's Use of Classical Mythology', p. 89.

Romanticism, his realist texts tell a story with deep reflection on the human situation. Dostoevsky profoundly influenced Western literature with his fiction framed in existentialism. His writings were intricately linked to his time as he witnessed the gradual passing of the Great Russian Empire.

Inspired by the writings of Voltaire, Kant and Hegel, Dostoevsky was a writer steeped in philosophical thought. With his keen insight into the human psyche he developed characters related to the theory of psychology later expounded by Sigmund Freud. We must remember that he had a tyrannical father and experienced hardship and suffering in prison. While incarcerated, it was his Christian faith that kept Dostoevsky sane and saintly. Orthodox Christianity is a distinctive feature of Russian identity. The Orthodox Church played a prominent role in Russia's public and political life. Critical of Catholicism, Dostoevsky espouses the Orthodox concept of *sobornost* or spiritual harmony in *The Brothers Karamazov*.

Traditional Catholic literature seeks to illustrate the truth of the faith with its emphasis on Church teaching and doctrines. Graham Greene represents a new kind of Catholic writing, filled with biblical imagery and sacramental symbolism, to reveal his vision of life. His purpose in drawing upon elements of Catholicism in his writing is more to enhance the intensity of his narrative than to enlighten his readers. Greene's novels do not attempt to portray an idyllic life of faith but to present the moral and spiritual struggles of the individual in a hostile world. While we can trace elements of Christianity in his writings, we also witness the close relation between the sacred and secular realms. There is thus a rapprochement with secularity in his religious narrative.

Given his critical attitude towards institutional religion, Greene's relationship with the Catholic Church was rather ambivalent. The depiction of his main protagonists in *The Power and the Glory* reveals the conflict between the Christian community and a godless regime bent on eradicating the Church. There is irony and even comic relief in *The Power and the Glory*, which non-Catholics may not grasp. Be that as it way, his treatment of theological issues facilitates a dialogue between the Church and the modern world.

As we have seen, there is an interactive relationship between Christianity and Western literature. The fall and redemption motif frames poems, prose and plays. At the same time, Western literary tradition has influenced how the gospel vision is translated into society. In many literary works religious truth is more effectively communicated through language and literary form than through the Church.

# Bibliography

Agajanian, Shaakeh, 'Problem of Hamlet: A Christian Existential Analysis', *Religion in Life* 46, no. 2 (1977), pp. 213-24

Alighieri, Dante, *The Divine Comedy*. Digital Dante Edition with Commento Baroliniano, https://digitaldante.columbia.edu/dante/divine-comedy/

Aquinas, Thomas, 'Whether Sin Incurs a Debt of Punishment Infinite in Quantity?', in *The Summa Theologica*, 1a2ae.87.4, tr. Fathers of the English Dominican Province (New York: Benziger Bros, 1947), https://www.ccel.org/a/aquinas/summa/FS/FS087.html#FSQ87A4THEP1

Augustine, *City of God*, book 19, chapter 21. https://www.newadvent.org/fathers/120119.html

Augustine, *City of God*, tr. William M. Green. Loeb Classical Library 417 (Cambridge, MA: Harvard University Press, 1972)

Augustine, *Enchiridion on Faith, Hope, and Love* (Grand Rapids, MI: Generic NL Freebook Publisher, 1999)

Auweele, Dennis Vanden, 'Existential Struggles in Dostoevsky's *The Brothers Karamazov*', *International Journal for Philosophy of Religion* 80, no. 3 (2016), pp. 279-96

Bakhtin, Mikhail, *Problems of Dostoevsky's Poetics,* ed. Caryl Emerson (Minneapolis: University of Minnesota Press, 1984)

Baldridge, Cates, *Graham Greene's Fictions: The Virtues of Extremity* (Columbia, MO: University of Missouri Press, 2000)

Barineau, R. Maurice, 'The Triumph of Ethics over Doubt: Dostoevsky's *The Brothers Karamazov*', *Christianity and Literature* 43, no. 3/4 (1994), pp. 375-92

Barolini, Teodolinda, *Dante and the Origins of Italian Literary Culture* (New York: Fordham University Press, 2006)

Barolini, Teodolinda, '*Inferno* 13: Non-Dualism; Our Bodies, Our Selves', in *Commento Baroliniano*, Digital Dante (New York: Columbia University Libraries, 2018) https://digitaldante.columbia.edu/dante/divine-comedy/inferno/inferno-13, no. 5

Barth, J. Robert, *Coleridge and Christian Doctrine* (Cambridge, MA: Harvard University Press, 1969)

Baxter, Jason M., *A Beginner's Guide to Dante's Divine Comedy* (Grand Rapids, MI: Baker Academic, 2018)

Beauregard, David N., 'New Light on Shakespeare's Catholicism: Prospero's Epilogue in *The Tempest*', *Renascence* 49, no. 3 (1997), pp. 159-74

Beauregard, David N., '"Great Command O'Ersways the Order": Purgatory, Revenge, and Maimed Rites in *Hamlet*', *Religion and the Arts* 11, no. 1 (2007), pp. 45-73

Benson, Sean, 'The Resurrection of the Dead in *The Winter's Tale* and *The Tempest*', *Renascence* 61, no. 1 (2008), pp. 3-24

Berdyaev, Nicholas, 'The Grand Inquisitor: Christ and Antichrist', in Fyodor Dostoyevsky, *The Grand Inquisitor*, ed. Jerry S. Wasserman (Columbus, OH: Charles E. Merrill Pub. Co., 1970), pp. 68-76

Bergonzi, Bernard, *A Study in Greene: Graham Greene and the Art of the Novel* (Oxford: Oxford University Press, 2008)

Blanco Sarto, Pablo, 'Dostoevsky Overcomes Nihilism: Luigi Pareyson Reads *The Brothers Karamazov*', *Wrocławski Przegląd Teologiczny* 29, no. 1 (2021), pp. 393-411

Boone, Mark J., 'The Role of Platonism in Augustine's 386 Conversion to Christianity', *Religion Compass* 9, no. 5 (2015), pp. 151-61

Bosco, Mark, 'From *The Power and the Glory* to *The Honorary Consul*: The Development of Graham Greene's Catholic Imagination', *Religion and Literature* 36, no. 2 (2004), pp. 51-74

Bosteltter, Edward E., 'The Nightmare World of *The Ancient Mariner*' (1962), in Alun R. Jones and William Tydeman (eds.), *Coleridge: The Ancient Mariner and Other Poems; a Casebook* (London: Macmillan, 1973), pp. 184-99

Boulger, James D. '*The Rime of the Ancient Mariner* – Introduction', in Boulger (ed.), *Twentieth Century Interpretations of The Rime of the Ancient Mariner* (Englewood Cliffs, NJ: Prentice-Hall, 1969), 16-17.

Boulger, James D. (ed.), *Twentieth Century Interpretations of The Rime of the Ancient Mariner: A Collection of Critical Essays* (Englewood Cliffs, NJ: Prentice Hall, 1969)

Brink, J. R., '*Paradise Lost* as Literary Myth', *Cithara* 22, no. 1 (1982), pp. 13-21

Brown, Peter, *Augustine of Hippo: A Biography* (Berkeley-Los Angeles: University of California Press, 1967)

Buchan, A. M., 'The Sad Wisdom of the Mariner', in James D. Boulger (ed.), *Twentieth Century Interpretations of the Rime of the Ancient Mariner* (Englewood Cliffs, NJ: Prentice-Hall, 1969), 97-98

Camus, Albert, *The Rebel: An Essay on Man in Revolt* (New York: Vintage International, 1991)

Cervigni, Dino S., 'The Muted Self-Referentiality of Dante's Lucifer', *Dante Studies with the Annual Report of the Dante Society* 107, no. 107 (1989), pp. 45-74

Chadwick, Henry, *Augustine of Hippo: A Life* (Oxford: Oxford University Press, 2009)

# Bibliography

Chernaik, Warren, 'God's Just Yoke: Power and Justice in *Paradise Lost*', in Chernaik, *Milton and the Burden of Freedom* (Cambridge: Cambridge University Press, 2017), pp. 143-71

Chernaik, Warren, 'Monarchy and Servitude: The Politics of *Paradise Lost*', in Chernaik, *Milton and the Burden of Freedom* (Cambridge: Cambridge University Press, 2017), pp. 124-42

Cloete, Nettie, 'Religious Paradoxes in Graham Greene's Novels', *Koers* 63, no. 4 (1998), pp. 313-25

*Code of Canon Law*. https://www.vatican.va/archive/cod-iuris-canonici/eng/documents/cic_lib3-cann747-755_en.html#BOOK_III

Cohen, Sharon, '"Balaam's Ass": Smerdyakov as a Paradoxical Redeemer in Dostoevsky's *The Brothers Karamazov*', *Christianity and Literature* 64, no. 1 (2014), pp. 43-64

Coleridge, Samuel Taylor, 'The Destiny of Nations. A Vision', https://internetpoem.com/samuel-taylor-coleridge/the-destiny-of-nations-a-vision-poem/

Coleridge, Samuel Taylor, *The Rime of the Ancient Mariner: Complete, Authoritative Texts of the 1798 and 1817 Versions with Biographical and Historical Contexts, Critical History, and Essays from Contemporary Critical Perspectives*, ed. Paul H. Fry (Boston: Bedford/St Martin's, 1999)

Collett, Jonathan Howard, 'Milton's Use of Classical Mythology in *Paradise Lost*', *PMLA: Publications of the Modern Language Association of America* 85, no. 1 (1970), pp. 88-96

Coonradt, Nicole M., '"To Be or Not to Be?": Hamlet and Tyrannicide', *Religion and the Arts* 25, no. 3 (2021), pp. 243-62

Coursen, Herbert R., *The Tempest: A Guide to the Play* (Westport, CT: Greenwood Press, 2000)

Cox, John D., 'Recovering Something Christian about *The Tempest*', *Christianity and Literature* 50, no. 1 (2000), pp. 31-51

Coyle, John Kevin, *Manichaeism and its Legacy*, Nag Hammadi and Manichaean Studies 69 (Leiden and Boston: Brill, 2009)

Cunningham, David S., '*The Brothers Karamazov* as Trinitarian Theology', in George Pattison and Diane Oenning Thompson (eds.), *Dostoevsky and the Christian Tradition* (Cambridge: Cambridge University Press, 2001), pp. 134-55

Daiches, David, *Milton: Paradise Lost* (London: E. Arnold, 1983)

Danielson, Dennis Richard, 'The Contexts of Milton's Theodicy', in Danielson, *Milton's Good God: A Study in Literary Theodicy* (Cambridge: Cambridge University Press, 1982), pp. 1-23. doi:10.1017/CBO9780511735646.002

David, Aers, and Bob Hodge, '"Rational Burning": Milton on Sex and Marriage', in *Paradise Lost: John Milton*, ed. William Zunder (New York: St Martin's Press, 1999), pp. 67-87

Dodds, E. R., 'Tradition and Personal Achievement in the Philosophy of Plotinus', *Journal of Roman Studies* 50, no. 1-2 (1960), pp. 1-7

Dostoevsky, Fyodor, *The Brothers Karamazov: The Constance Garnett Translation Revised by Ralph E. Matlaw; Backgrounds and Sources, Essays in Criticism* (New York: Norton, 1976)

Dostoyevsky, Fyodor, *The Grand Inquisitor*, ed. Jerry S. Wasserman (Columbus, OH: Charles E. Merrill Pub. Co., 1970)

Dowling, Paul M., '*Paradise Lost* and Politics Gained: Milton Rewrites Scripture', *Cithara* 44, no. 2 (2005), pp. 16-31

Dreher, Diane Elizabeth, 'Milton's Warning to Puritans in *Paradise Lost*: Another Look at the Separation Scene', *Christianity and Literature* 41, no. 1 (1991), pp. 27-38

Earl, James W., 'The Typology of Spiritual Growth in Augustine's *Confessions*', *Notre Dame English Journal* 13, no. 2 (1981), pp. 13-28

Engell, James, 'Biographia Literaria', in Lucy Newlyn (ed.), *The Cambridge Companion to Coleridge* (Cambridge: Cambridge University Press, 2002), pp. 59-74

Fallon, Stephen M., '*Paradise Lost* and the Materialism Debate', *Continuum* 3 (1994), pp. 174-203

Feuerbach, Ludwig, and George Eliot, *The Essence of Christianity; by Ludwig Feuerbach; by Marian Evans*, 2nd ed. (New York: Calvin Blanchard, 1855). Nineteenth Century Collections Online. https://link.gale.com/apps/doc/CGYVFR144757537/NCCO?u=cuhk&sid=bookmark-NCCO&xid=ae97cb65&pg=33

Finn, James, 'Graham Greene as Moralist', *First Things*, no. 3 (1990), pp. 20-29

Fiore, Peter Amadeus, *Milton and Augustine: Patterns of Augustinian Thought in Paradise Lost* (University Park, PA: Pennsylvania State University, 2022)

Fish, Stanley Eugene, *Surprised by Sin: The Reader in Paradise Lost* (London: Macmillan, 1967)

Forsyth, Neil, 'Satan', in Louis Schwartz (ed.), *The Cambridge Companion to Paradise Lost*, Cambridge Companions to Literature (Cambridge: Cambridge University Press, 2014), pp. 17-28

Foster, Kenelm, *The Two Dantes, and Other Studies* (Berkeley, CA: University of California Press, 1977)

Fulford, Tim, 'Slavery and Superstition in the Supernatural Poems', in Lucy Newlyn (ed.), *The Cambridge Companion to Coleridge* (Cambridge: Cambridge University Press, 2002), pp. 45-58

Gaston, Georg, *The Pursuit of Salvation: A Critical Guide to the Novels of Graham Greene* (Troy, NY: Whitston Pub. Co., 1984)

Gibson, A. Boyce, *The Religion of Dostoevsky* (Philadelphia: Westminster Press, 1973)

Goodley, Nancy C., 'Thy Kingdom Come: The Eschatological Vision of The Tempest', *Religion in Life* 45, no. 2 (1976), pp. 238-46

Grayson, Cecil (ed.), and University of Oxford Dante Society, *The World of Dante: Essays on Dante and his Times* (Oxford and New York: Clarendon Press, 1980)

Greenblatt, Stephen, *Hamlet in Purgatory: Expanded Edition* (Princeton, NJ: Princeton University Press, 2013)

# Bibliography

Greene, Graham, *The Power and the Glory* (New York: Penguin Classics, 2003)

Guardini, Romano, *The Conversion of Augustine* (Westminster, MD: Newman Press, 1960)

Guardini, Romano, 'The Legend of the Grand Inquisitor', *Cross Currents* 3, no. 1 (1952), pp. 58-86

Guite, Malcolm, *Mariner: A Voyage with Samuel Taylor Coleridge* (London: Hodder & Stoughton, 2017)

Gurung, Jeevan, 'Coercion and Conversion Using Christian Magnanimity in Shakespeare's *The Tempest*', *Papers on Language and Literature* 55, no. 4 (2019), pp. 347-67

Hall, Grace R. W., *The Tempest as Mystery Play: Uncovering Religious Sources of Shakespeare's Most Spiritual Work* (Jefferson, NC: McFarland & Co., 1999)

Harrison, Carol, *Rethinking Augustine's Early Theology: An Argument for Continuity* (Oxford and New York: Oxford University, 2006)

Hill, Christopher, '*Paradise Lost* and the English Revolution', in William Zunder (ed.), *Paradise Lost: John Milton* (New York: St Martin's Press, 1999), pp. 15-27

Hollander, Robert, 'Milton's Elusive Response to Dante's Comedy in *Paradise Lost*', *Milton Quarterly* 45, no. 1 (2011), pp. 1-24

Hollingworth, Miles, *Saint Augustine of Hippo: An Intellectual Biography* (London: Bloomsbury Publishing, 2013)

Holmes, George, 'Dante and the Popes' in Cecil Grayson (ed.), *The World of Dante: Essays on Dante and his Times* (Oxford and New York: Clarendon Press, 1980), pp. 18-43

Hruska, Anne, 'The Sins of Children in *The Brothers Karamazov*: Serfdom, Hierarchy, and Transcendence', *Christianity and Literature* 54, no. 4 (2005), pp. 471-95

Jasper, David, 'The Priest in the Novels of Graham Greene', *Theology* 124, no. 2 (2021), pp. 84-92

Jensen, Steven J., *Sin: A Thomistic Psychology* (Washington, DC: Catholic University of America Press, 2018)

Kanevskaya, Marina, 'Smerdiakov and Ivan: Dostoevsky's *The Brothers Karamazov*', *The Russian Review* 61, no. 3 (2002), pp. 358-76

Kelly, David F., 'Sexuality and Concupiscence in Augustine', *Annual of the Society of Christian Ethics* 3 (1983), pp. 81-116

Kennedy, Robert Peter, Kim Paffenroth and John Doody, *Augustine and Literature*, Augustine in Conversation (Lanham, MD: Lexington Books, 2006)

Kierkegaard, Søren, and Walter Lowrie, *For Self-Examination and Judge for Yourselves! And Three Discourses, 1851* (Princeton, NJ: Princeton University Press, 1944)

Labriola, A. C. 'John Milton', *Encyclopedia Britannica*, 5 December 2021, https://www.britannica.com/biography/John-Milton

Leah, Gordon, 'A Bad Priest? Reflections on Regeneration in Graham Green's Novel *The Power and the Glory*', *Heythrop Journal* 51, no. 1 (2010), pp. 18-21

Le Goff, Jacques, *The Birth of Purgatory* (Chicago: University of Chicago Press, 1983)

Levy, Eric P., 'The Mind of Man in *Hamlet*', *Renascence* 54, no. 4 (2002), pp. 219-33

Levy, S. M., 'Coleridge's *Rime of the Ancient Mariner*: Theodicy in a New Key', *Anglican Theological Review* 78, no. 2 (1996), pp. 206-24

Lew, Ji-Whang, 'Free Will, Self-Consciousness, and the Spiritual Journey of Conversion: St. Augustine and Friedrich Schleiermacher on the Origin of Sin', *Journal of Korean Christian Theology* 25 (2002), pp. 93-112

Lewis, C.S. *A Preface to Paradise Lost* (London: Oxford University Press, 1960)

Lieu, Samuel N. C., *Manichaeism in the Later Roman Empire and Medieval China*, 2nd ed., revised and expanded ed., Wissenschaftliche Untersuchungen Zum Neuen Testament 63 (Tübingen: J.C.B. Mohr, 1992).

Link, Christopher A., 'Bad Priests and the Valor of Pity: Shusaku Endo and Graham Greene on the Paradoxes of Christian Virtue', *Logos* 15, no. 4 (2012), pp. 75-96

Marrs, Oral John, 'Of "Minimal Religion," a Mystical Discourse on Orthodox Spirituality in the Life, Discourses, and Sermons of Father Zosima, in Book Six of *The Brothers Karamazov*', *St Vladimir's Theological Quarterly* 61, no. 4 (2017), pp. 411-26

Martindale, Charles, *John Milton and the Transformation of Ancient Epic* (London: Croom Helm, 1986)

McGann, Jerome J., 'The Ancient Mariner: The Meaning of the Meanings', in McGann, *The Beauty of Inflections: Literary Investigations in Historical Method and Theory* (Oxford: Clarendon Paperbacks, 1988), pp. 134-72

McGrath, Alister E., *Christian Literature: An Anthology* (Oxford: Blackwell Publishers, 2001)

McHale, Heather Moreland, 'Graham Greene's Pope: Finding God in Battered Places', *America* 213, no. 15 (2015), pp. 22-24

Milton, John, *Paradise Lost*, introduced by Philip Pullman (Oxford: Oxford University Press, 2005)

Mong, Ambrose, *Christianity in the Modern World: A Study of Religion in a Pluralistic Society* (Cambridge: James Clarke & Co., 2021)

Montemaggi, Vittorio, 'Love, Forgiveness, and Meaning: On the Relationship between Theological and Literal Reflection', *Religion and Literature* 41, no. 2 (2009), pp. 79-86

Moores, Donald J., '"Oh Happy Living Things": Healing Serpent Power in Coleridge's "Rime"', *Studies in Spirituality* 17 (2007), pp. 225-46

Morson, Saul Gary, 'Fyodor Dostoyevsky', *Encyclopedia Britannica*, 7 November 2022 https://www.britannica.com/biography/Fyodor-Dostoyevsky (7 November 2022)

# Bibliography

Myers, Benjamin, *Milton's Theology of Freedom* (Berlin: Walter de Gruyter, 2006)

Namli, Elena, '*The Brothers Karamazov* and the Theology of Suffering', *Studies in East European Thought* 74, no. 1 (2022), pp. 19-36

Naumann, Marina Turkevich, 'Death in *The Brothers Karamazov*', *St Vladimir's Theological Quarterly* 25, no. 3 (1981), pp. 159-74

Newlyn, Lucy (ed.), *The Cambridge Companion to Coleridge* (Cambridge: Cambridge University Press, 2002)

Newman, John Henry, 'Lectures on the Doctrine of Justification', *Newman Reader,* http://www.newmanreader.org/works/justification/lecture4.html

Newman, John Henry, 'Sermon 6 – On Justice, as a Principle of Divine Governance', *Newman Reader,* http://www.newmanreader.org/works/oxford/sermon6.html

Newman, John Henry, 'Sermon 24 – The Religion of the Day', *Newman Reader,* http://www.newmanreader.org/works/parochial/volume1/sermon24.html

O'Donnell, James J., 'The *Confessions* of Augustine: An Electronic Edition', https://faculty.georgetown.edu/jod/conf (24 November 1999)

Oort, J. van, 'The Young Augustine's Knowledge of Manichaeism: An Analysis of the *Confessions* and Some Other Relevant Texts', *Vigiliae Christianae* 62, no. 5 (2008), pp. 441-66

Ortiz, Jared, *'You Made Us for Yourself': Creation in St Augustine's Confessions* (Minneapolis, MN: Fortress Press, 2016)

Panichas, George A., 'Fyodor Dostoevsky and Roman Catholicism', *Greek Orthodox Theological Review* 4, no. 1 (1958), pp. 16-34

Pareyson, Luigi, 'Pointless Suffering in *The Brothers Karamazov*', *Cross Currents* 37, no. 2/3 (1987), pp. 271-86

Pattison, George, and Diane Oenning Thompson, *Dostoevsky and the Christian Tradition* (Cambridge: Cambridge University Press, 2001)

Pellow, C. Kenneth, 'The "Presence" of Dostoevsky in Graham Greene's *The Power and the Glory*', *Renascence* 67, no. 1 (2015), pp. 57-74

Perkins, Mary Anne, 'Religious Thinker', in Lucy Newlyn (ed.), *The Cambridge Companion to Coleridge* (Cambridge: Cambridge University Press, 2002), pp. 187 -99

Pryce-Jones, David, *Graham Greene* (Edinburgh: Oliver, 1963)

Rahv, Philip, 'The Legend of the Grand Inquisitor', in Fyodor Dostoyevsky, *The Grand Inquisitor*, ed. Jerry S. Wasserman (Columbus, OH: Charles E. Merrill Pub. Co., 1970)

Reist, John S., 'Reason as a Theological-Apologetic Motif in Milton's Paradise Lost', *Canadian Journal of Theology* 16, no. 3-4 (1970), pp. 232-49

Rist, John M., 'Augustine on Free Will and Predestination', *Journal of Theological Studies* 20, no. 2 (1969), pp. 420-47, http://www.jstor.org/stable/23960142

Ritchie, Daniel, and Jared Hedges, 'Choosing Rest in *Paradise Lost*', *Christianity and Literature* 67, no. 2 (2018), pp. 271-93

Rookmaaker, Hendrik Roelof, *Towards a Romantic Conception of Nature: Coleridge's Poetry up to 1803: A Study in the History of Ideas* (Amsterdam: John Benjamins Publishing Co., 1984)

Samuel, Irene, *Dante and Milton: The Commedia and Paradise Lost* (Ithaca, NY: Cornell University Press, 1966)

Sauter, Gerhard, and John Barton, *Revelation and Story: Narrative Theology and the Centrality of Story* (Aldershot: Ashgate, 2000)

Schwartz, Louis (ed.), *The Cambridge Companion to Paradise Lost* (New York: Cambridge University Press, 2014)

Shakespeare, William, *Hamlet,* ed. Burton Raffel (New Haven, CT, and London: Yale University Press, 2003)

Shakespeare, William, *The Tempest*, ed. Virginia Mason Vaughan, and Alden T. Vaughan (Walton-on-Thames: Thomas Nelson, 1999)

Sheed, Foley J., *Confessions,* 2nd ed., with notes, by Michael P. Foley (Indianapolis, IN: Hackett Publishing Co., 2006)

Short, Edward, 'John Henry Newman in the "Realms of Superstition"', *Newman Studies Journal* 12, no. 2 (September 2015): 46-75

St Amant, Clyde Penrose, 'God Gets His Man: A Study of Graham Greene', *Perspectives in Religious Studies* 1, no. 1 (1974), pp. 55-61

Stevenson, Warren, *A Study of Coleridge's Three Great Poems: Christabel, Kubla Khan, and The Rime of the Ancient Mariner* (Lewiston, NY: Edwin Mellen Press, 2001)

Stoeber, Michael, 'Mysticism in *The Brothers Karamazov*', *Toronto Journal of Theology* 31, no. 2 (2015), pp. 249-71

Stuart, J. A., 'The Augustinian "Cause of Action" in Coleridge's *Rime of the Ancient Mariner*', *Harvard Theological Review* 60, no. 2 (1967), pp. 177-211

Sutherland, Stewart R., *Atheism and the Rejection of God: Contemporary Philosophy and the Brothers Karamazov* (Oxford: Blackwell, 1977)

Taylor, Janet, 'The *Confessions* of St Augustine: A Spiritual Classic', *Crux* 21, no. 3 (1985), pp. 17-27

Thompson, Diane Oenning, 'Problems of the Biblical Word in Dostoevsky's Poetics', in George Pattison and Diane Oenning Thompson (eds.), *Dostoevsky and the Christian Tradition* (Cambridge: Cambridge University Press, 2001), pp. 69-99

Thorpe, Vanessa, 'How Rome Tried to Censor Greene's Masterpiece', *The Guardian,* https://www.theguardian.com/uk/2001/jul/08/books.humanities

Tiffany, Grace, '*Hamlet*: Reconciliation and the Just State', *Renascence* 58, no. 2 (2005), pp. 111-33

Tikannen, Amy, 'Graham Greene', *Encyclopedia Britannica*, 13 May 2023, https://www.britannica.com/biography/Graham-Greene.

Took, John, 'Ecclesiology on the Edge: Dante and the Church', *Studies in Church History* 48 (2012), pp. 65-82

Troyan, N., 'The Philosophical Opinions of the Petrashevsky Circle', *Philosophy and Phenomenological Research* 6, no. 3 (1946), pp. 363-80

Turner, James, *One Flesh: Paradisal Marriage and Sexual Relations in the Age of Milton* (Oxford: Clarendon Press, 1987)

Urban, David V., 'The Falls of Satan, Eve, and Adam in John Milton's *Paradise Lost*: A Study in Insincerity', *Christianity and Literature* 67, no. 1 (2017), pp. 89-112

Urban, David V., 'Prospero, the Divine Shepherd, and Providence: Psalm 23 as a Rubric for Alonso's Redemptive Progress and the Providential Workings of Prospero's Spiritual Restoration in Shakespeare's *The Tempest*', *Religions* 10, no. 8 (2019), pp. 1-16

Warren, Robert Penn, 'A Poem of Pure Imagination: An Experiment in Reading', in James D. Boulger (ed.), *Twentieth Century Interpretations of The Rime of the Ancient Mariner: A Collection of Critical Essays* (Englewood Cliffs, NJ: Prentice Hall, 1969), pp. 21-47

Wood, Lawrence, 'Seeing with a Thousand Eyes', *The Christian Century* 122, no. 10 (2005), pp. 37-43

Yu, Anthony C., 'Milton's Epic Motives: On the Formative Principles of *Paradise Lost* as Poetic Theodicy', *Criterion* 8 (Spring 1969), pp. 26-34

Zunder, William, *Paradise Lost: John Milton* (New York: St Martin's Press, 1999)

Zysk, Jay, 'In the Name of the Father: Revenge and Unsacramental Death in *Hamlet*', *Christianity and Literature* 66, no. 3 (2017), pp. 422-43

# Index

Adam and Eve 8, 19-20, 40, 74-75, 79, 83, 85-86, 91
albatross 96-97, 101-103, 105-108, 110, 112
Ambrose St., 5, 7, 11-13, 15, 127, 152
angels 9, 33, 38-39, 47, 74, 77, 81-82, 84, 86-88, 103
anti-clericalism 147
Aquinas, Thomas 27, 30 34, 43, 47, 53-55, 152
Archetypal Characters 137
Ariel 64, 66-68
Aristotle 27, 48, 54
atheism 36, 110, 120-124, 129, 136
Augustine, St. 1-3, 5-25, 27, 30-32, 38, 73, 80-83, 87, 91, 93, 106-107, 119, 127, 132, 152
autobiography 6-7, 16-17

bad priest 141, 148-149
Bakhtin, Mikhail 114
Barth, Karl 87
Beatrice 29, 44-46, 153
Benedict XVI, Pope 49
Berdyaev, Nicholas 129
Bernard of Clairvaux, St. 46
*Brothers Karamazov, The* 3, 113, 116, 119, 128, 132, 144, 149, 155
Buddhism 7

Caliban 64, 66-68
Catholicism 25, 62, 116, 126-130, 133-134, 136, 140, 155
Cato of Utica 42
Celestial Rose 46-47
Chrysostom, St. 2

City of God, The 32, 80-83
Claudius 51-52, 54-55, 58-63
Coleridge, S.T. 3, 95-97, 99-100, 104, 106-110, 112-113, 154
colonialism 100
Communism 140
concupiscence 22-23
*Confessions* 3, 5-7, 12, 15-18, 22, 32, 106-107, 131, 141-142, 152
contrapasso 32, 89
cosmogony 8
Creatio ex Nihilo 17
creation 3, 7-8, 10-11, 16-18, 39, 75, 77, 91, 97-98, 106, 109-110, 112-113, 122-124, 152
Cyprian, St. 6

Dante Alighieri ix, 3, 26-49, 57, 74, 88-89, 91, 152-153
disobedience 23, 75, 77, 79-80, 82-83, 85, 92, 109
*Divine Comedy, The* ix, 3, 26, 28, 31-32, 49, 57, 73, 89, 152-153,
Donatism 5
Dostoevskian Echoes 144
Dostoevsky, Fyodor 3, 113-122, 124-132, 144, 155
dualism 12-13, 15-16, 24, 118

Eden 29, 75-76, 80, 89, 94, 154
Elects 8
Elizabethans 55, 61
Endo, Shusaku 135
Enlightenment 6, 154
Enneads 14

Epicureans 36, 38
evil ix, 8-11, 14-16, 20-23, 30-31, 33, 38-39, 41-42, 54-55, 57-59, 73-76, 78-82, 86, 91-92, 96-97, 99, 106-107, 109, 115-116, 118-123, 125, 129, 133, 135, 144-145, 148-149
ex opere operato 142

Fall and Redemption 3, 96, 106, 113, 120, 143, 155
Feuerbach, Ludwig 87, 128
forgiveness 3, 51, 56, 60, 62-65, 67-72, 109, 112, 121, 125, 134

gnostic 5, 7, 9
Grand Inquisitor 117, 124-126, 128-131, 144-145, 149
Greene, Graham 3, 133-137, 140-144, 146-151, 155
Guardini, Romano 126

hagiographies 3
*Hamlet, The Tragedy* 3, 50-63, 69, 72, 91, 153
heaven 3, 17, 27, 31-32, 39, 45-46, 48, 59-61, 63, 67, 69, 74, 77, 79, 87-91, 93, 100, 103, 133-134, 139, 144, 149
hell 3, 27-33, 35-36, 38-39, 41-42, 47-48, 58, 61-63, 76, 87-91, 121, 133-134, 136-137, 153
heresy 12, 24 ,36, 87, 150
heterosexuals 41-42
Hilary of Poitiers, St. 6
Holy Office 150-151
Holy Spirit 12, 17, 35
Homer 1, 23, 27, 44, 48, 74
homosexuals 41-42

idolatry 111
imagery 72, 115, 143, 153-155
*Inferno* 27-29, 31, 34, 37-38, 42, 46, 48, 88-91, 152

Jerome, St. 2, 6, 48, 127
Judas 38, 119, 138, 140
Jung, Carl 108-109
Justin Martyr, St. 6, 87

Kierkegaard, Søren 55-56

leprosy 99-100
Lewis, C.S. 2
lieutenant 136, 140, 142-147
Limbo 27, 29, 45, 48-49
logic 126
*Logos* 14, 96
Lucifer 38-39, 90
Lucy, St. 43

Mani 7-9, 12
Manichaeism 5, 7-12, 15, 25, 38, 152
Manichaean dualism 13, 15-16, 24
martyrdom 6-7, 135, 141
Mexico 135-136, 141, 143
Michael, Archangel 79-80, 84-85, 93
Milton, John 3, 73-76, 78-86, 88-94, 153-154
Monica, St. 5, 15, 21
monotheism 108-109
Moses 66, 74, 152
mythology 43, 153

Neo-Platonism 7, 13-15, 20, 24, 152
Newman, John Henry 110-111
New Testament 13, 87, 149, 154
Nietzsche, Friedrich 88

Old Testament 7, 13, 27, 48, 59, 65-66, 74, 91, 97, 148
Origin of Evil 9, 91, 106
Original Sin 19-20, 23, 25, 93, 106-107
Orthodox Church 115, 127-130, 155

pagan writings 1-2, 153
papal infallibility 127-128
*Paradise Lost* 3, 73-74, 77, 80-82, 86-87, 90-94, 153-154
*Paradiso* 27-28, 44-46
paradox 78, 147-149
patriarchs 48
Paul VI, Pope 28, 151
Paul, St. 1-2, 7, 12-13, 16, 18, 21, 24, 60, 69, 142, 148
Peter, St. 28, 35
Plato 1, 13-14, 48
Platonists 13-15, 24
Plotinus 14, 19
Polonius 51-53, 55
polytheism 14, 109

# Index

*Power and the Glory, The* 3, 133-136, 141-144, 148-151, 155
pride 9, 22, 24, 30, 38-41, 43, 77, 81, 83, 90, 118-119, 130, 138-139, 147-148
priesthood 135, 140, 142, 147-149
Prometheus Bound 91
Protestantism 130
*Purgatorio* 27-28, 34, 39-40, 43-44, 46, 152
purgatory 3, 27-29, 39-44, 47, 54-55, 57-58, 61-64, 137, 152-153

Rahner, Karl 149
Raphael, Archangel 76-77
Redemption 3, 24, 91, 93, 96, 102, 106, 109, 112-113, 120-121, 134, 143, 149, 155
Renaissance 3, 86, 153
Resurrection 27, 37, 48, 69-71, 112, 118, 121, 151
*Rime of the Ancient Mariner, The* 3, 95, 154
Romantic Movement 95, 154
Romanticism 154-155
Russia 114-116, 122, 127-128, 131-132, 144, 154-155

sacraments 62, 142, 146, 150
salvation 11, 13-14, 27, 61-63, 68, 74, 77, 92-93, 96, 102, 112, 118, 123, 126, 130, 135, 137, 151
Satan 29, 73-77, 79, 81-93, 109, 130, 154
Scorsese, Martin 135
Shakespeare, William 3, 50-51, 53, 57, 59, 64-65, 67, 69-73, 153
Shelley, P.B. 2
Siberia 115, 117-118, 120, 126
Simon Magnus 35

sin 3, 7, 10, 12, 14, 16, 18-20, 22-25, 27, 29-30, 32-36, 38-41, 43, 45, 48, 55, 58, 60, 62, 63, 67-68, 73, 77, 79-85, 88-89, 93-94, 96, 100, 103, 106-107, 109-110, 112, 120, 134-135, 137-138, 140, 148-149, 151-152,
socialism 3, 126, 128-129, 136
soliloquy 56, 76, 91
*sorbornost* 116, 130
suffering 3, 6, 12, 37, 58, 62, 69, 76, 93, 108, 115, 120-124, 126, 136, 139, 145, 149, 155
superstition 110-112, 136

*Tempest, The* 3, 50-51, 63-70, 72, 153
temptations 6, 125, 129, 131, 136, 140
Tertullian 2, 87, 141
Trinitarian Theology 131
Trinity 6, 13-14, 17-18, 24, 38, 46, 113, 131, 136
tyranny 37, 54, 80

Ultramontanism 127-128

vices 30, 32, 36, 43, 55, 100
Virgil 27-29, 33, 36, 41, 43-45, 48-49, 74, 90, 152-153
virtues 40, 45-46, 64, 82
voluntas 31
von Baltasar, Hans Urs 45, 69

Whisky Priest 136, 140-143, 147, 151
Wordsworth, William 2, 95

Zoroastrianism 7